# CULTURAL HISTORY OF BENGALI PROVERBS

# CULTURAL HISTORY OF BENGALI PROVERBS

**Sudeshna Basak**

GYAN

First Published in Bengali by
Ananda Publishers Pvt. Ltd. in 2007

Cultural History of Bengali Proverbs

Rs. 630



ISBN: 978-81-212-1028-7



Published in 2010 in India by
Gyan Publishing House,
23 Main, Ansari Road, Darya Ganj,
New Delhi-110002
Phones : 23282060, 23261060
Fax : 011-23285914
E-mail: books@gyanbooks.com
Website: www.gyanbooks.com
*Translated by* : Sumanta Sen

*Laser Type Setting by*: Quick Media, Delhi
*Printed at* : Young Art Press, Delhi

*Dedicated to my grandfathers*
*Late Radhagobinda Basak*
*Late Tarunaditya Rakshit*

# Contents

# Preface

"Anybody with any experience of life must be aware of how these (proverbs) play an important role in character formation, in providing guidelines to everyday activities like agriculture and the influence of natural phenomenon like the rainfall. It will not be an exaggeration to suggest that it was the proverbs and the messages these sent out that helped a predominantly unlettered rural population with advice as to how to conduct daily affairs and lead a peaceful life".

These words of Sahityaratna Harekrishna Mukhopadhyay, whose name will ever be associated with Dr. Sushil Kumar De's collection of proverbs, indicate the inseparable nature of relationship between the Bengali and the proverb. They are an integral part of our literary and cultural tradition, the preservation of which had been greatly emphasised by Rabindranath Tagore. The poet had insisted that such preservation and study would open the doors towards self-discovery and an effort towards reaching that goal has been made in this volume. The purpose was not just to collect proverbs but to unveil their nature and variety, to identify their role in society both as a mirror and guide.

Proverbs of course had no specific space in Tagore's scheme of discovering folk traditions but there is ample evidence of his great interest in the collection and study of Bengali idiom. Manuscripts at Visva Bharati's Rabindra Bhavan contain, in the poet's handwriting, 78 specimens of such idiom. The 19th century also saw scholars from abroad collecting proverbs of whom special mention must be made of William Morton and James Long. Indians like Nilratna Haldar, Rangalal Bandyopadhyay, Kanailal Ghosal, Dwarkanath Bosu, Madhumadhab Chattopadhyay and later Sushil Kumar De and Harekrishna Mukhopadhyay also came forward and collected thousands of Bengali proverbs.

The work by no means is over. From Caryapada, Sri Krishna Kirtan to Bharatchandra and the writers of today, proverbs and sayings have been widely used and the volume has dealt with them as also proverbs in some poems. So far there has been no effort at a full investigation into the subject and this is what I have sought to attempt.

I must take the opportunity to thank many individuals and institutions both in India and Bangladesh without whose help this work would not have been completed. Those who deserve special mention are Professor Ashraf Siddiqui, Professor Wakil Ahmed, Professor Biswanath Roy, Professor Manas Mazumdar, Dr. Dulal Chowdhury and Sunil Chandra Basak. I am grateful to Professor Anisuzzaman for carefully going through the manuscript despite his busy schedule. My relationship is so close with Sumit Kumar Basak, who constantly encouraged me, that a formal thank you is not needed. Of the institutes mention must be made of Bangla Academy, Dhaka, Visva Bharati, Santiniketan, National Library, Kolkata, libraries of the Dhaka University and Sishu Academy, Bangiya Sahitya Parishad and also the central and Bengali department libraries of Kolkata University. Lastly who can ignore the constant encouragement from Ishtiaq Hasan, Dr. Asma Begum, Parichay (Sunny) and Abhinandan (Ani), Sri Nivas and Bindiya of Bengaluru and my two sons Subhechha (Prince) and Rebanta (Raj).

My special thanks are due to Hindol Bhattacharyya for reading the proofs and much more.

The Gyan Publishing House has kindly taken all measures to bring out this book in a befitting form for which I remain grateful.

August, 2009

Dehradun 248006 **Sudeshna Basak**

# 1

# Proverb : Definition and Nature

An accepted definition of proverb is that it is a "saying, usually short, that expresses a general truth about life."[1] It is born out of man's experience and attains a kind of universality as it reflects values developed through the ages. Reflecting, as it does, the culture of people, it brings home in an attractive manner, tales, beliefs and thoughts. Thus its use is so common in everyday life.

The 'Proverb' is the shortest and most witty expression of the experiences of a community. As Archer Taylor has said, "A proverb is a terse, didactic statement that is current in tradition or, as an epigram says, the wisdom of many and the wit of one"[2]. To American sociologist Alan Dundes, a proverb "appears to be a traditional, prepositional statement consisting of at least one descriptive element, a topic and a comment."[3] Drawing from his own experience a person may make a significant statement which gets repeated by others and with time is accepted by society as a proverb. So even if it is the product of individual experience, it gradually gets to become the property of the entire community.

Being a product of experience, a proverb is born more in the mind than in the heart, it is cerebral in nature. The words of course have a literal meaning which, however, conveys little. The essence of a proverb lies in the secondary meaning and thus both its creation and understanding involves a process of intellection. And it is the female mind that finds easy expression through proverbs. As Dr Sushil Kumar De has so succinctly put it: "The special characteristic of the Bengali proverb lies in the ease with which the language of the kitchen has passed on to the male world, like *'tele begune jwale otha'* (getting worked up like brinjals in a frying pan) *'machher tele machh bhaja'* (frying fish in its own oil), *chhai phelte bhanga kulo* (odd job man). These are witty expressions of a woman's daily experience, brought out of the narrow confines of the inner chambers."[4]

The proverb is akin to the adage but is more tightly knit. Born out of long experience it is recognized as an adage, as are the sayings attributed to the woman known as Khana, but are actually products of keen observation of human life and its surroundings.

Every country has its own proverbs. These may not have much literary merit but provide invaluable insight into folk culture. Thus they are useful ingredients of any literary work and at the same time provide the needed signals in a man's daily life. Some examples will help to illustrate the point:

(a) *hathi kaday padle masha machhio lathi mare*
elephant stuck in mud is kicked even by flies and mosquitoes.

The proverb illustrates the pitiable condition of a fallen hero.

(b) *sandhle jamai kanthal khay na, pagade giye paiti chate*

son-in-law refuses the jackfruit only to go the dung heap to suck its skin.

Not accepting something when offered and to search is vain later.

(c) *yar kaj tar chinta nai, parha padshir ghoom nai*
neighbour more worried than he who is really concerned.

Proverb on undue interference in others' affairs.

(d) *yadi hay sujan, tentul patay nayjan*

if friend then a tamarind leaf will hold nine

The proverb illustrates the point, united we stand.

(e) *sabure meoa phale*

wait and the fruit will grow

Proverb advocating patience—slow and steady wins the race.

A few proverbs of other states and of different countries along with their Bengali counterparts and meaning are following :

Tamil : *akkal irukki twarai tan machchan urbu*
Bengali : *meye banchle jamaier adar*
If the daughter lives, the son-in-law is feted- no flowers to tend if the tree dies.

Kannar : *pramanikathaiei mukh bhada aneka dosagalen muchu thayedi*
Bengali : *nirdosh drishti anek trutir abaran*
Innocent look covers many faults

Gujarati : *sati ditayani ma jhanpe futay*
Bengali : *sakaler kaj karur ekar kaj nay*
Community works is no personal show

Oriya : *Chali na jani batar dosh*
Bengali : *nachte na janle uthaner dosh*
Poor workman blames his tools

English : after clouds comes fair weather
Bengali : *dukher pare sukh*
Italian : absence is the enemy of love
Russian : you look for the horse you ride on
Latin : no one knows what he can do till he tries
French : who acts not when he should, acts not when he would
German : less advice and more hands
Spanish : when the rabbit has escaped, comes advice
Danish : no answer is also an answer
Japanese : applause is the root of abuse
Japanese : old men are twice children
Herbrew : youth is a garland of roses, age is a crown of thorns
Arabian : the barber learns to shave on the orphan's face
Chinese : one word will not settle a bargain
American : big smoke, small fire

Such proverbs abound all over the world. A striking feature of proverbs is the manner in which the state in one or two lines the lesson learnt from long observation. The statement is terse and intelligent if properly used, a proverb helps avoid a lengthy exposition of a point that is being sought to be made. Not only that, a proverb helps even unlettered women in rural areas to drive home their contention without going through the trouble of making a speech. Thus:

*ma nai yar*
*na nai tar*

('na' in colloquial Bengali is boat). The literal meaning of the proverb is, he who does not have a mother does not have a boat, the clear purpose being to highlight the plight of a motherless child. The boat here is a symbol of shelter which the motherless child does not enjoy.

The proverb expresses truth. Even the simplest truth is expressed through the proverb of which it has been said, "the truth or fact concealed in the proverb is often so simple and ordinary that it is akin to a platitude." Many feel that it is this simplicity that makes essential such garnishings as humour, often coarse, rhythm, alliteration etc and come to the conclusion that the proverb is essentially rustic wit and buffoonery presented in a shiny package. In Bengal such an attitude stems from a lack of knowledge of language and humour or the desire to be unduly finicky. While it is true that a Bengali proverb often carries a touch of somewhat rough humour, it is at the same time not essential for all proverbs to be heavily garnished and alliteration and rhythm, though popular, are not essential ingredients. Nor would it be correct to suggest that the proverb is of a piece with rustic coarseness. Born in villages the proverb does have an element of bucolic wit but this is to be seen in proverbs all over the world. Yes, the language is strong and forthright but this is the language of daily use, it cannot be seen in isolation from the experience of everyday life. Of the English proverb it has been said, "Most of the coarsest proverbs are typically English".[5] The same is true in case of the Bengali proverb.

It is not possible to comprehend the true meaning of a proverb without a close association with the environment in which it is born. The same proverb, used in a different context may, as Mazhrul Islam has said have a different meaning. For instance:

*bhatarer nai adar*
*mukhe day chadar*

not having husband's love
covers face with wrapper

This simple meaning changes, however, when the proverb is applied in the context of two women wrangling with each other. One married woman may well make fun of the other with the proverb which in this case means, 'she can show only her wrapper but not her husband's love'. This clarifies the contextual meaning of a proverb.

There are some proverbs which are strictly regional, not to be heard elsewhere. Besides this, there are some regional proverbs which can be heard in other regions being spoken in the language of that particular region. In the case of some regional proverbs, the meaning goes beyond the boundaries of that region. Like:

(a) *hathi kaday padle byango lathi mare*
elephant caught in a bog is kicked even by the frog

(b) *ye randhe se ki chul bandhe na*
doesn't she who cooks tend her hair
(Preoccupation with one work is no excuse for not doing another)

(c) *yar shil tari noda/tari bhangi danter goda*
break his teeth with his own grinder
(To attack a man with his own weapons)

(d) *bhaba majilo mon/kiba hadi kiba dom*
where emotion has softened the mind
who bothers about caste
(Love is blind and lovers cannot see)

(e) *shakun kande gorur shoke*
vulture weeps for the dead cow
(shedding crocodile tears)

(f) *yar biya tar khabar nai*
*pada padshir ghoom nai*
not bothered is the girl to be married
neighbours losing sleep
(Interfering in others' affairs)

(g) *ma pay na khata silai karar suto*
*cheler paye choddo sikir juto*
mother has no thread to stitch
son wears costly shoes
(what is seen is not the real picture appearance belies the truth)

(h) *nei kaj to khoi bhaj*
no work so fry parched rice
(Doing things not needed)
*yeman buno ol*
*teman bagha tentul*

(i) strong tamarind to match the wild plant
(measure for measure)

(j) *ki katha bolbo sai*
*panta bhate tak dai*
what do I say
sour curd on watered rice
(Too absurd for words)

Some of the proverbs, having the same meaning are found in varying form in different districts of Bangladesh. Thus the proverb, habits die hard is expressed through the same symbol of a dog's tail remaining curled despite all efforts to straighten it but in different ways in Chittagong, Sylhet, Rangpur and Manikgunj.

Therefore, irrespective of provincial and geographical borders, proverbs remain unaltered.

The original source of the proverb was spontaneously expressed in the minds of people. As the origination of the proverb was very much spontaneous, so it has been used in the verbal expression of the people, retaining its spontaneity. The meaning is not always the same, it can have more than one meaning depending on usage. As Dr Mazhrul Islam has said: "Like all other proverbs existing all over the world, the Bengali proverb also generally carries two meanings within itself. One meaning emerges from a reading of the proverb, the other lies concealed, the proverb can be interpreted in many ways. The reason for this is that of all the ingredients of the folklore, the proverb has the greatest utility, its functions are the most. This function depends on the context".[7]

The use of the proverb is as old as the spoken word. It has great value in every day but that value is not of a fundamental nature as it is in the case of a moral saying, a maxim. The proverb does not aim at any moral upliftment nor does it propose to educate. The proverb does have a fundamentality of its own but that is not as an indicator of any fundamental truth. Thus "good is bound to prevail" may be true in moral sense but perhaps not so in the everyday world. Similarly *yamn, jamai, bhaga, teen nay apna* (the yam, son-in-law and sister's son can never be your own) may have been born out of daily experience but is certainly not a moral saying. The inspiration behind the proverb is not morality but common knowledge, not an abstract thought but a direct experience. That what is seen everyday and known may not be the Truth but it is that which in most cases gives birth to the proverb. The truth concealed in the proverb is not the truth of theory but of information. The proverb is essentially realistic, its power of easy communication is one of the reasons why it does not pass into oblivion.

The general characteristics of proverb are:

(1) Long experience of a people, maturity, aphorisms are expressed through it.

(2) The sentences are short and transparent. Examples, sarcasm, epigram, exaggeration, ornamentation find expression in a proverb.

(3) It is in the language of the ordinary. There is no room for loose construction, redundant words.

(4) It is an advice imparted in an easy, humorous manner. Emotion gains precedence over language.

Some proverbs to illustrate the above points:

(a) *bojhar upar shaker anti*
bunch of creepers on a huge bundle
(last straw on the camel's back)

(b) *lebu anek chatkale tita hope yay*
much squeezed lemon turns bitter
(a point should not be pressed too far)

(c) *Yam, jamai, jamindar, teen nay apnar*
yam, son-in-law and landlord can never be your own

(d) *dekhte na parle hantan byanka*
can't stand him (her) so say he (she) walks crookedly
(to find imaginery faults with a disliked person)

(e) *oti lobhe tanti nashta*
too much greed destroys the weaver
(killing the goose that lays the golden egg)

(f) *asal ghare mashal nai*
*dhenkir ghare bati*

no light in the main room
lamp lights the threshing floor
(waste of resource)

Every language has certain phrases which resemble proverbs but are actually not so. These are known as proverbial phrase and like the proverb are marked by paucity of words and depth of meaning. These have become an intrinsic part of the Bengali language and particularly household language. Such as:

*kana-kodi* — cowrie with a hole, useless as it cannot be converted (had its origin when the cowrie was legal tender).

*chhaier gada*— ash heap, garbage dump

*chhoonch-chaluni* — needle and sieve both having holds and skin to each other.

*handi-sara* — pitcher and plate, the two representing all kitchen items.

*dhan-chal* — paddy and rice

Such proverbial phrases are drawn from practically every sphere of domestic and social life. Some more examples of phrases which are very commonly used and are derived from popular sedentary games:

*Poabaro* — a particular throw of the dice which brings unexpected luck.

*Tekka deoa* — to throw the ace and win the hand, to triumph over others.

*Hater panch* — a card that is held back for the last, the last resort.

*Kistimat* — cheak mate

Then there is,

*agadh jaler machh* — deep water fish

and

*alpa jaler lanka* — chillie floating in a little water, a person of small means.

Many proverbial phrases have been drawn from the mythologies, Ramayana and Mahabharata:

*Kumbhakarner nidra* — deep sleep like that of Ravana's brother Kumbhakarn who slept for six months at a stretch.

*Gokuler shand* — like the proverbial bull, useless.

*Agastya yatra* — a journey of no return like that of the sage Agastya.

*Jadabharat* — One without any sense.

*Hariharatma* — kindred souls.

*Lankakanda* — a tumultuous affair, resembling the fire at Ravana's Lanka.

| | | |
|---|---|---|
| *Kurukshetravyapar* | — | a battle like that at Kurukshetra. |
| *Dhanukbhanga pan* | — | grim determination |
| *Dvata Karna* | — | as generous as Karn in Mahabharata |

Not only mythology but contemporary history also found its way in some proverbial phrases. Thus:

| | | |
|---|---|---|
| *Mager Mullook* | — | land of the Mags, the wild people of the Arakan hills; a state of lawlessness. |
| *Dine dakaiti* | — | daylight robbery, something which was common during the last days of Muslim rule. |
| *Husein Shaher amol* | — | the days of Husein Shah's rule, a period of peace and order. |
| *Dhan hante Mahipaler geet* | — | singing the praise of King Mahipal while husking paddy; beating around the bush—there is another variation in which Lord Shiva replaces Mahipal. |

Proverbial phrases featuring individuals and places:

| | | |
|---|---|---|
| *Kalighater kangali* | — | beggars always to be found around the famous Kali temple at Kalighat. |
| *Dhapdhara Govindhapur* | — | a place largely inaccessible. |
| *Gourchandrika* | — | also beating around the bush. |
| *Harighosher goal* | — | literally the cowshed of Hari Ghosh, an open house. |
| *Lage taka debe Gouri Sen* | — | a reference to the generosity of a rich man, actually money that need not be accounted for. |

Such phrases were also born out of an observation of individuals and also the community:

| | | |
|---|---|---|
| *kunde kishan amabasya khoje* | — | lazy peasant looks for the moonless night. |
| *gharmukko bangali* | — | homebound Bengali, reflecting his supposed dislike of venturing out. |
| *bheto bangali* | — | rice eating Bengali, indirect reference to idle nature. |
| *ranmukho sepai* | — | sepoy looking for a fight, a man itching for a fight. |
| *gamla chore gangapar* | — | crossing the Ganga in a bucket, trying to do the impossible. |

There are phrases of two more words acting as a metaphor. Like :

| | | |
|---|---|---|
| *Amabasyar chand* | — | moon on a moonless night, something that cannot be there. |
| *chinir balad* | — | bullock carrying sugar bags, labouring towards an end which bring no benefit personally. |
| *akash kusum* | — | flowers in the sky, wild dreams. |
| *aday kanchkalay* | — | ginger and green banana, two which are opposed to each other. |
| *adajal* | — | ginger and water, trying hard to achieve something. |

Then there are the proverbial comparisons:

| | | |
|---|---|---|
| *rakter matan lal* | — | as red as blood. |
| *kaker mata dhurta* | — | as cunning as the crow |

*naba durbadal shyam* — as green as the new grown grass.

*kokiler matan kantha* — voice as that of the cuckoo

*dudher mata sada* — as white as milk.

**The Sayings of Khana, Dak, Ghagh and Proverb**

These sayings, or *bachan*, constitute complete sentence. So does the proverb and both are statements on behalf of the whole society. In Bengal there are various such sayings attributed to Khana, and also sayings known as *daker bachan* and are related to farming. The *ghagher bachan* are heard in Bangladesh and are associated with Varahamihir, the famous astronomer of yore. These, however, cannot be called proverbs. Though both are derived from the experience of everyday life, the *bachan* lacks the humour of the proverb.

The sayings of Khana are about the weather and agriculture and are known as Weather Proverbs. Of all the sayings, these are most in use. The ones about agriculture were perhaps collected by a learned woman, Khana, though there is a little historical evidence of this. Perhaps 'Khana' is a variant of the term *'kshan'* which means time and many of the sayings indicate the time most appropriate for the cultivation of different crops. Also if Khana was actually the daughter-in-law of Varaha and the wife of Mihir, as is popularly believed, then the sayings would have been heard all over India and not just in Bengal, Orissa aned Assam. This is because of the similar weather conditions in the three states.

If the rains in the month of Baisakh then the aus paddy enjoys a good harvest. Hence Khana's saything:

*Baisakher pratham jale*
*aus dhan dwigum phale*

In the first rain of Baisakh
Aus paddy doubles itself

The sayings take into account stellar positions and advice is given about the most propitious time of farming. Besides this, month and seasonwise weather conditions, also, are found in Khana's Bachan. The advice to farmers take into account the difference months and seasons. So:

*dodal kudule megher ga*
*madhye madhye dichchhe ba*
*balade chasay bandhte al*
*aj na hay tabe kal*

the rumbling of the clouds
hitting now and then the spade and axe
time for work for bullock and farmer
if not today then tomorrow

The saying specify the exact time for sowing different crops:

*patal bunle phalgune*
*phal bare dwigune*
*phalgune na bunle ol*
*seshe hay gandagol*
*khana bale chashar po*
*sarater seshe sarisha ro*
*sarisha bune kalai moog*
*bane bedao chapode buk*
*kartiker uno jale*
*duno dhan khan bale*
*tamak ponto gundiye mati*
*beej ponto guti guti*
*hat bishek kari phank*
*am kanthal punte rakh*
*gachh gachhali ghana sabena ba*
*phal tate phalbe na*
*khana bale suno suno*
*sarater seshe mula buno*

sow pulbul in falgun
crop will double itself

if ol (a vegetable) not sown in falgun
there will be problems later
Khana says, 'O farmer,
plant mustard at the end of Sarat (Autumn)
pulses after mustard
go beat your chest in the forest
short spell of rain in kartick
doubles the paddy
crush soil and plant tobacco
leave space and plant mango and jackfruit
trees close together
won't get fruits
Khana says, listen
plant raddish after autumn

The sayings of Khana were once very popular. Some more examples of advice, both agriculture related and otherwise:

*deke deke khana gan—rode dhan chhayay pan*
khana sings—paddy in the sun, betel leaves in shade

*sravaner puro bhadrer baro-er madhye yato paro*
grow as much as possible in Shravan (rainy season) and twelve days of bhadra (the next month when monsoon starts to fade away)

*gachh, gachhali ghana sabe na—gachh habe ta phal habe na*
trees not close together—trees may grow but not fruits
*sap, shala, zemindar—teen nay apnar*
snake, brother-in-law, landlord, three can never be your own

*randhi, badi, nari, purusher age khay*
*bhara kalsir jal ar tarase shukay*
woman who cooks and eats before husband
has her pitcher full of water dry up in fear

*mangshe mangsha baday*
*ghee badayh bal*
*dudhe labla bade*
*shage bade mal*

meat helps grow meat
ghee (clarified butter) increases strength
milk lends grave
creepers clean bowels

Just as Khana's sayings deal with famine, rain, drought, so also do they give advice on which month is good for a particular crop. Such as, if the south wind blows in the rainy month of asadh then floods will take place. Or, just as the Brahmin priest leaves when given his fees so do the rains end with the southern wind. Again,

*chaite thar thar*
*baisakhe jhad pathar*
*jaisthe tara phute*
*tabe janbe barsha bate*

oppressive heat in chaitra
storm and hailstorm in baisakh
stars in jaistha
all indicate rains

*madhumase pratham dine hay sei bar*
*rabi seshe, mangal bares, durbiksha budhbar*
*som sukhra guru ar*
*prithvi say na sasyer bhar*
*panch sani pay meene*
*sakuni mangsa na khay ghune*

If the first day of the month of chaitra is a sunday, there will be draught. If it is Tuesday, there will be rain. If it is Wednesday, there will be famine and if the month begins on a Monday or Thursday or Friday, then there will be plenty of crops. In case, Chaitra has five Saturdays, there will be famine.

Farming, Khana says, must be started on an auspicious day (suvakshan) and on the way to the field, the farmer should not listen to any bad news or *asuva barta.* Reaching the field he should start work from the east. These instructions, if followed, will bring in a bumper harvest.

There are instructions also on months in which particular crops should be sown:

*patal bunle Phalgune phal bade dwigune*—pulbul in Phalgun will double the crop.

*khana bale shun shun, sarater seshe mula bun*—Khana says plant raddish at the end of autumn.

*akh, ada, puin, a teen chaite rui*—sugarcane, singer and the puin creeper in chaitra.

For turmeric the sowing months are baisakh and jaistha and for mustard the end of autumn. About fertilizers, Khana says,

*manush mare yate, gachhna sare tate*—that which kills man cures trees.

What is Khana's advice to those building a house?

*pube hans, paschime banka, uttare kala, dakshine mela*

*dakshine chhede, uttare bede, ghar karge pota jude*

A duck pond in the east, banana and bamboo in the north and west so that the north wind cannot enter.

That saying of Khana which rural Bengali has believed the most is regarding childbirth. Count the words making up the name of the village, that of the pregnant women and that of a flower which she will utter during the preparations for the child's delivery. Add the figure, divide the total by three and if the result is one then a boy will be born and a daughter is the result is two of the result is zero then three will be a miscarriage. Though totally unscientific, yet, once it was considered true by villagers.

Then there are the sayings known as *daker bachan.* These also deal essentially with the weather and farming operations which is natural considering the age in which they were born. Thus:

*yadi barshe kati*
*laiya yay nati*

if it in kartick
takes away grandson

*yadi barshe agane*
*raja yay magane*

if it rains in aghrayan
king goes begging

*yadi barshe poushe*
*agun lage tushe*

if it rains in poush
the rice bran catches fire

*yadi barshe maghe*
*agun lage bage*

if it rains in magh
orchards catch fire

*yadi barshe magher sesh*
*dhanya rajar punya desh*

if it rains in the end of magh
glory to the king and country is blessed

These sayings appear to be expressions of general belief born out of popular experience and acquired a definite structure at a time when the Aryan languages were coming up in the country.

*ame dhan*
*tentule ban*

mangoes bring paddy
tamarind flood

*ushayoge ye jan yay*
*dak bale siddhi se pay*

he who ventures out at dawn
dak says success comes his way

*swami seva sanjher bati*
*dak bale lakshmir jhampi*

husband's care, lighting evening lamp
dak says (opens) treasure chest of Lakshmi

These are also wise sayings and may help sociologists in their studies:

*murkha put nashta stree*
*er chaite kashta ki*

stupid son, unfaithful wife
what can bring more pain than this

Also indicators of good and bad:

*pingal ankhi chapal ati*
*ostha dagar alakshan ati*

brown eyes, very fickle
thick lips, bad women

Some broad conclusions can be arrived at about the dak sayings:

(1) The first collection of such sayings, *Dakarnab*, is available.

(2) The sayings gained circulation thanks to roving minstrels and got assimilated into regional languages and transformed.

(3) Though principally concerned with agriculture, the sayings also indicate the time for social occasions like marriages. These paint a picture of the social and economic conditions of ancient Bengali and Assamese societies.

(4) At times these also reflect Buddhist rites and morals. Also with the spread of Islam, Arabic and Persian worlds found their way to the sayings,

(5) In his 'Dohakosh' Sarhopa made some critical comments about certain superstitions of his him. Support for these can be had in the dak sayings.

(6) The proverb is a reasoned argument. The dak saying has little time for reason and logic.

Some similarities can be noticed in the dak sayings and those of Khana. For instance, both insist that dawn is when the birds cry out but do not fly out of their nests.

The sayings of Ghagh are popular in Bangladesh. Like Khana Ghagh is also associated with Varahamihir. Some of the sayings attributed to him are also to be found in the Hindi speaking areas categorized as follows:

Concerning agriculture
Concerning time
Concerning measurement
Concerning systems
Concerning rainfall
Concerning irrigation
Concerning fertility

The sayings seek to establish that farming is the best occupation and suggests:

Land must be tilled with own hands.

Cultivation must be intensive with the help of good irrigation.

The sayings also advice on the best location of a farm, the qualities of a good farmer, the best time for sowing and harvesting, the consequences of untimely sowing, the indications of rain and draught, the effects of weather on crops and animals. These also deal with the time of ripening of different crops, the distance to be kept between two crops, the importance of fertilizer and the needs of different crops, cattle feed and the quality of milch cattle as well as the best time for buying and selling.

Though differences persist about treating such sayings as proverbs, the ones of Khana are still used in every day conversation in the manner as proverbs even if these are not referred to as such. The sayings of Khana and dak are indeed rich with directions for the welfare of society and with lessons drawn from everyday experience.

In the context of this discussion, it will perhaps not be out of place to take a look at the study of proverbs in this country.

William Morton, a priest, published a collection of proverbs in 1832 which was called, *A Collection of Proverbs, Bengali and Sanskrit, with their translations and applications in English*. Nilratna Sharma's *Kavita Ratnakar*, a collection of Sanskrit proverbs, had of course appeared earlier.

The man who is recalled even today with great reverence in this connection is Reverend James Long. In 1868-69 was published from Calcutta in two volume his, *Prabadmala or two Thousand Bengali Proverbs illustrating native life and feelings*. Earlier, in 1851, had come out his *Bengali Proverb*, a collection of five thousand women (proverbs which he had collected roaming the countryside; his two other important works were, *Oriental Proverbs in relation to folklore and Sociology, with suggestions for their collections, interpretation and publication* (1875) and Eastern Proverbs and Emblems which came out in 1881.

Around the same time as Long, the Commissioner of Chittagong Hills, Captain T.H. Lewin, came out with his *Hill Proverbs of the inhabitants of the Chittagong Hill Tracts* in 1873. Another civilian J.D. Anderson published in 1897 a collection of 352 proverbs of the Chittagong region.

A collection of Bengali proverbs was published by *Bamabodhini*, edited by Umeshchandra Dutta, in 1886. In 1890 a similar collection was published by Kanailal Ghosal and titled *Parbad Samgraha*. Prabodh Chandra Mazumdar's Bangiya *Prabachanabali* was published in 1892 in the journal *Ugrakshatriya Pratinidhi* of Calcutta. Dwarkanath Bosu's *Prabad Pustak* came out next year—divided in two parts, the book dealt with theory of proverbs and proverbs.

Collections of proverbs and books on the subject continued to be published. Inspired by Rabindranath, Abdul Karim collected a number of Chittagong proverbs and in 1909, at the fourth annual meeting of the Bangiya Sahitya Parishad, Sailesh Chandra Mazumdar read a paper on proverbs.

A collection particularly worth mentioning was that published by Dr. Sushilkumar De in 1352 of the Bengali calendar. His book *Bangla Prabad* contains 10,600 proverbs as also a scholarly discussion on the subject. Dr. Asutosh Bhattacharya's *Bangla Lok Sahitya* also deserved special mention as it has further advanced the study of proverbs in Bengal.

Among other efforts that need to be mentioned are, Dr. Enamul Huq's *Chattagrami Banglar Rahasyaved*, Mohammed Hanif Pathan's *Bangla Prabad Parichiti* and Dr. Dulal Chowdhury's *Chakma Prabad*, a collection of proverbs of the Chakma tribals of the Chittagong Hill Tracts.

## References

1. Martin H. Manser: Proverbs, New Delhi, 2005, p. 1.
2. Taylor Archer: SDFML, edited by Maria Leach, New York, 1984, p. 902.
3. Dandes Alan: 'On the Structure of the Proverb,' 1981, p. 601. The Wisdom of Many, Ed. Mirdw and Alan Dundes, New York.
4. De, Sushilkumar: Bangla Probad, 1401, p. 26.

# 2

# Varieties of Bengali Proverbs

Like all folk creations, the proverb can be divided into two categories, literary and popular. The categories of course do not stand apart, the popular of folk proverb often finds its way into literary works. Most literary proverbs are also, like the others, a part of the oral tradition that marks folk culture. Some examples:

(1) *apna mangse harina bairi*

deer's meat makes it its enemy

This is taken from the Caryapada. The deer is killed for its flesh and that makes it an enemy of itself.

(2) *bamon haiya hat baraile sashi*

dwarf reaching for the moon

This is taken from Kabikankan Mukundaram Chakrabarty's 'Chandimangal' which means, seeking to attain the impossible. The non-literary of popular version is, *bamon haye chande hat.*

(3) *ami to chhai felte bhanga kulo achhi*

I am the broken winnow to gather up the ash.

Found in Dinabandhu Mitra's play, *Biye Pagla Budo,* or Marriage-crazy Old Man. The proverb refers to an useless person who can be made to do all kinds of dirty work.

(4) *meye to nay aguner phulki*

not a girl but a spark of fire

Used in Amritlal Bose's play Nabayauban or Fresh Youth and means a tomboy or sharp talking girl.

(5) *bhanga handi joda lage na*

broken pot cannot be mended

From Sarat Chandra Chattopadhya's novel *Mejdidi* to mean what is done cannot be undone

(6) *nengtir abar bakheya silai*

fancy stitch for a loincloth (backeya is one such stitch)

It means poor cannot afford luxuries and was used by Kazi Nazrul Islam in his poems.

The folk proverbs can be divided into several sub-categories:

1. Concerning deities
2. Concerning mythological characters.
3. On historical personalities.
4. Relating to social life.
5. Relating to the family.
6. Concerning the human body.
7. Concerning habits and customs.
8. Relating to domestic items.
9. Relating to nature: (a) plant life and (b) stellar world.
10. Concerning agriculture.
11. Concerning food.
12. Concerning animals and insects.
13. Relating to musical instruments.
14. On luxury item.
15. On love.
16. On place names.
17. Relating to folk tales.
18. On folk education.
19. On folk decisions.

20. On folk journalism.

21. Miscellaneous.

**Concerning Deities**

If God created Man in his own image, then in people's minds, the deities also acquire human forms and qualities. There has never been any end to man's curiosity about the deities who had been featured in the epics and the *puranas* and with time proverbs came to represent ideas about the deities, the manner of their worship and the results of such worship. Sometimes such proverbs are respectful and at other times mixed with scorn. And always the deities are portrayed as human, as part of the living world.

**Bhagwan** : The Almighty God whom the faithful always look up for succour. Thus:

(a) *bhakter bhagwan abhagter apaman*
God is for the believer, worth nothing to the non-believer.

(b) *bhoger karta bhagwan*
God provides food for all.

(c) *yar keu nei tar bhagwan achhe*
He who has none has God

(d) *manuser deoa kulay na*
*bhagwaner deoa phuray na*

What man gives is not enough
What God gives is unlimited.

**Siva** : Also known as Mahadeva, Siva is, with Vishnu and Brahma, lord of the deities, a symbol of renunciation and at the same time of creation and destruction. Imagined as one with matted hair and with snakes adorning his body, there are many proverbs around him:

*Siver mathay narkel phatana*
Breaking coconut on Siva's head

Siva's worship involves bathing him in coconut water and the proverb suggests a simple mode of worship.

*sapke marle sivake lage*

Kill snake and hurt Siva

The proverb means, one cannot be hurt without hurting another.

*dub diey jal khele Siver bap ter pay na*

If you take water on the sly even Siva won's know.

During Siva's worship even the drinking of water is taboo but if that is done on the sly then nobody can find out, not even-Siva. In short, done in the quite, the deed remains unknown.

*Bish kheye Biswamvar*

Swallow poison and sand save the world

Siva was supposed to have done that and the proverb denotes a person who has become immune to attacks.

**Siva and Parvati :** Parvati is Siva's wife and inseparable from him. So:

*Siva nache ronge, Parvati nachey sange*

Siva dances in joy and Parvati dances with him

**Salgram Sila :** Salgram is a dark, round stone which is supposed to symbolize Narayan and is worshipped in homes.

The proverbs related to this have their funny side:

(a) *Salgramer shoa basa saman*
It is the same whether the salgram is sitting or lying down

(b) *Mani to salgram na mani to pathar*
Faith makes it a salgram, otherwise a stone

(c) *sab nudi salgram hay na*
all stones are not salgram

(d) *salgramer dhan bhana*
salgram husking paddy—something impossible

**Hari** : The redeemer, without his help man cannot survive. The proverb brings out his various qualities:

(a) *Hari yar sakha bal, dusman tar tal*

he who has Hari as friend, has enemies under his feet.

(b) *vrindavane achhen hari, ichha haleo roite nari*

Hari in Vrindavan, can't be with him despite wishes.

(c) *haripade thake mon, hriday majhe Vrindavan*

Surrender to Hari and Vrindavan is in the heart.

(d) *hari bachan pran, baidyar bodol man*

Hari saves life, physician enjoys prestige.

(e) *parer karta Hari deben charan tari*

Hari rules the world and helps entry to next

(f) *rakhe Hari make Ke*?

If Hari protects, who can kill?

**Krishna** : Incarnation of Vishnu. Proverbs highlight his supreme powers:

(a) *Krishna katha madhurbani, tumi bolo ami suni*

Krishna's words are like nectar, say and I will listen.

(b) *rakhe Krishna mare ke, mare Krishna rakhe Ke*

If Krishna saves who kill, if Krishna kills who can save.

(c) *gachher Phool sri krishnay namah*

Dedicate the flowers in trees to Krishna

Proverb means that is the only way to save them.

(d) *kaker mukhe Krishna katha*

Crow speaking the words of Krishna

Proverb to describe something wholly improbable.

**Jagannath** : Deity without arms, incarnation of Krishna and at time an object of innocent fun. A visit to his temple at Puri is considered a must by devout Hindu as :

*yogir chinta Jagannath, fakirer chinta Mecca*
Yogi dreams of Jagannath and fakir of Mecca

Proverb draws attention to the single minded devotion of the religious, irrespectice of faith.

*apna hat Jagannath, parer hat ento pat*
Proverb means, depend on your own ability

*kalo handi keyapat, tabe dekhbi Jagannath*
black pots and keya leaves, then Jagannath

Proverb refers to the place around the Puri temple littered with pots and leaves in which pilgrims have cooked and eaten.

**Kartick :** Son of Siva and Parvati. It is believed that barren women can have children if he is worshipped and this belief has been made fun of in the proverb:

*habe na ar banjar chhele kartick re tor bap ele*

The barren won't give birth Kartick even if your father comes—despite best efforts.

**Visvakarma :** Master craftsman, engineer. Proverb, however, makes fun of his abilities by referring to Jagannath's deformity:

*visvakarma kata karigar ta Jagannathey dekha gechhe*

How great is Visvakarma can be judged by looking at Jagannath

Another, however, shows respect:
*visvakarmar beta biyallish karma*
Son of Visvakarma, capable of many deeds

**Durga :** Goddess who destroys evil. Her worship is the biggest even among the Bengali Hindus. The idol is made of straw and adorned with gorgeous ornaments and clothes. Proverb makes fun this stress on show and pomp:

*Hinduder dugga pujo*
*oporey chikan chikan bhitore khader bujo*

Durga worship of Hindus

Gorgeous outside, straw inside

The proverb is from Muslim dominated Bangladesh.

**Kali :** The dark goddess is the angry form of Durga and the proverb brings out this anger:

*raktadanti Kali*

Kali with blood red teeth

Another proverb preaches religious tolerance:

*Ram Rahim Kali, bhed karleyi moli*

Ram, Rahim Kali, seek to separate and suffer.

Worship of the goddess involved sacrifice of goats and it is joked that the worship is a mere excuse for killing the animals for meat. Proverb runs:

*kalir dohai diye pantha khaoa*

Invoking Kali to eat meat

**Kali and Siva :** Kali represents violence while Siva calm and meditative. Hence:

*kalir sova kare ashi, Siver sova kare sashi*

The sword adorns Kali, the moon Siva

**Ganga Devi :** Wife of Siva, she cleanses all by flowing down as the river worshipped by Hindus. The Ganga water is needed for any performance of religious rites, including the worship of the deity herself. Hence:

*ganga jale ganga puja*

Worship Ganga in Ganga water

Another proverb is:

*gangay mayla phelle gangar mahatmya kame na*

Rubbish in the Ganga does not lessen her qualities.

**Lakshhmi :** Goddess of wealth and is worshipped for that reason. Yet there is always the awareness that beauty and fortune have another side also. So :

*lakshmir ghare kalo pencha*

Dark owl in Lakshmi's room

The 'dark owl' symbolises ugliness and ill luck. The proverb illustrates the lesson learnt from experience that the good and the ugly exist together, are both parts of life.

The favours bestowed by Lakshmi should not be misused. Otherwise:

*handir Lakshmi shundir badiyay*

Lakshmi in the pot goes to the ale house
also
*hater Lakshmi paye thela*

Turning down favour which comes one's way and to keep Lakshmi intact

*lakshmi aste duare agar*

When Laksmi enters close the door

**Saraswati :** Deity of learning. She is the sister of Lakshmi and together they represent the twin virtues of beauty and scholarship:

*rupe Lakshmi gune Saraswati*

Beautiful as Laksmi, learned as Saraswati (the ideal women).

Or

*saraswati barputra*

Blessed by Saraswati (a learned man)

**Annapurna :** Deity who is worshipped as a provider of food. Yet even with food in the house men may cry out of hunger, a contradiction not unknown in human life:

*annapurna yar ghare se kande anner tare*

Annapurna at home yet cries for food

Also

*sakhyat Annapurna*

Annapurna incarnate

A women who provides food to all—Her genorosity is personified.

**Manasa :** Deity of Snakes, is vengeful and cruel. Smoke of any burning repellant makes her even more angry:

*akey ma manasa tay dhunor gandha*

As if manasa is not enough, the smell of repellant

In plain terms, adding fuel to fire.

## II
## Mythological Characters

From time immemorial people have been curious about the various characters in the Ramayana, Mahabharata and the *purana* and it was only natural that proverbs would be created around them. Not that these people, largely unlettered, had any direct knowledge about the characters as they have been portrayed in the epics, their ideas of them stemmed from the portrayals in *yatra* performances and narrations of balladeers. In all these a lot popular imagination came into play and hence the characteristics attributed to such men and women often varied from that in the original texts.

**Rama :** Revered as deity, he was shown as an ideal ruler under whom the kingdom prospered and nobody suffered. Hence an ideal state of affairs has come to be known as Ram Rajya or akin to the kingdom of Rama.

In that ideal kingdom even the poorest of the poor could look up to the king for succour. So,

*bhojane ambal, shayane kambal, marane 'ram bal*

at the time of death take the name of Rama which is as essential as a sour dish to end a meal and a blanket to sleep on.

On the eve of his coronation Rama had to go on exile for fourteen years. Hence the proverb, *kal ram raja have aj banabash* or tomorrow Rama will be king and today he goes on exile, to denote sudden change in fortune, for the worse.

Other proverbs on him are:

*Ram namey bhut palay*

Rama's name sends ghosts running.

*bhuter mukhe ram nam*

Ghost uttering Rama's name—instance of hypocrisy.

*Ramer Hanuman*

Rama's hanuman, a devoted follower.

*shaman damaney ravan raja, ravan damaney ram*

Ravana defeats enemies, Rama defeats Ravana. This is the proverb to illustrate Rama's prowess.

*ramey marleo morbo raveney marleyo morbo*

Whether Rama kills or Ravana, I will die

Proverb to highlight helplessness.

*yaha ram taha ayodhyay*

Ayodhyaya is where Rama is

Ayodhyaya was Rama's capital and proverb means without Rama there is nothing. Also, *shey ram nei shey ayodhyaya neit*, meaning, No Ayodhyaya without Rama, just as there cannot be Hamlet without the Prince of Denmark.

**Lakshman :** Brother of Rama, totally devoted to him and always held as an example of filial devotion. Proverbs seek to highlight this:

*Ram Lakshman dui bhai, rathey chare swargey yai*

Ram, Lakshman two brothers, go to heaven in a chariot

*Ramer bhai Rakshman, ar ki*

Like Lakshman, Rama's brother

The Ramayana speaks of Lakshman as a dutiful brother in law:

*devar laksman*

Brother-in-law like Lakshman

**Sita :** Wife of Rama who had shared her husband's

hardships, was taken prisoner by Ravana. After Rama had become king she was unjustly suspected of having been unfaithful to him and was asked to prove her purity. When she had been taken away by Ravana, Rama had sought and got help of monkeys to rescue her and thus the proverb:

*Sita hara hoye ramer bandare adar*

Losing Sita Rama had to coax monkeys

meaning, at times of need help is sought even from base creature.

Sita's life was one of sorrow. Hence:

*yabat sita tabat duksha*

*morle sita ghuchbe duksha*

Where there is Sita there is sorrow

Only death will remove all sorrows.

The love of Rama and Sita has been compared to that of **Radha and Krishna:**

*yeman rama teman sita*

*yeman kanu teman radha*

Rama and Sita like

Krishna and Radha

Sita also features in proverb meaning asking a stupid question about a situation of which everything is known:

*sat kanda ramayan pare sita kar baap*

asking whose father is Sita after reading all seven parts of Ramayana.

**Ravana** : Being the demon king of Lanka, he had ten heads, twenty hands and ears. To rescue Sita from him, Rama had to bridge the sea and hence the proverb:

*ravaner doshey hay samudra bandhan*

Ravana's fault caused sea to be bridged.

Ravana's downfall was brought about by brother Vivishana who turned as a traitor:

*gharvede ravana nashta*

Division at home destroyed Ravana

A large family is often described as *ravaner ghusti* or the family of Ravana.

Rama had destroyed Lanka and the analogy is drawn to denote total destruction in the proverb, *ravaner puri charkhar* or Ravana's home ravaged.

Ravana had dreams of building a staircase to heaven and hence the *ravaner swarger sinri* to describe something absurd.

**Surpanakha :** Ravana's sister was very proud of her position:

*amar bhai ravana raja ami surpanakha*

*dhara majhe emon jora parish yadi dekha*

I am Surpanakha, my brother king Ravana

Show if you can two such on earth

**Marich :** Loyal follower of Ravana who was caught in quandary when his master asked him to lure Sita to him. If he did he would be killed by Rama and if he did not Ravana would do the same. Hence:

*rama marleo morbo ravaney marleyo morbo*

Whether Rama or Ravana I will be killed for sure

Or

*egule ram pichhole ravana*

Rama in front Ravana behind

**Vivisana :** Ravana's brother who had betrayed him. Any betrayal is thus reflected in:

*gharer satru vivishana*

Vivishana, the enemy inside

**Kumbhakarna :** Another brother of Ravana who slept for six months in a year. It was almost impossible to wake him and this is referred to in the proverb:

*kumbhakarner nidrabhanga*

Waking up Kumbhakarna

**Sugriva :** King of the monkeys, devoted to Rama and a great fighter.

The proverb goes:

*akey ramey raksha nei tay sugriva dosar*

As if Rama is not enough there is also Sugriva

The proverb is used to mean double trouble.

There are similar proverbs based on characters from the Mahabharata. One of them was Bhisma, whose resolve, to remain celibate, none could break:

*bhismer pratigya*

Resolve of Bhisma

**Karna :** Brave warrior who was also famous for his generosity:

*gharete nahiko anna tabu datakarna*

No food at home yet Karna remains generous

In everyday parlance the proverb also quietly questions the wisdom of such generosity.

**Arjuna :** Third of the Pandava brothers, known for his valour. When in exile from his brothers he had taken the name Brihannala and had helped Prince Uttar to victory:

*Brihannala rathi yar parajay kotha tar*

No defeat for him whose charioteer is Brihannala

Again at the battle of Kurukshetra, Janardan or Krishna had been Arjuna's charioteer

*sakha yar janardan tar sathe ki saje ran*

Is it wise to fight him whose friend is Janardan?

**Duryodhan :** After his defeat in the hands of the Pandavas, Duryodhan hid himself in a lake creating a column of water around him. This seeking to protect oneself through deceit is brought out in the proverb:

*duryodhaner mata Jalastambha kore thaka*

Living like Duryodhan in a column of water

**Shakuni :** Being a maternal uncle of Duryodhan, he had defeated the Pandavas by using loaded dice in a game in order to help his nephew.

His low cunning is reflected in:

*duryodhaner shakuni mama*

Duryodhan's uncle Shukuni

**Shalya :** Another uncle of Duryodhan who had taken charge of his army after all the great generals had failed. Fun has been made of him in:

*chandra surya asta gyalo jonaki dhare bati*

*bhisma drona karna gyolo shalya hola rathi*

When Moon and sun have set, firefly now wants to light the path

Bhisma, Drona, Karna failed, now Shalya is the general.

**Daibaki :** Mother of Krishna who had to give him away at birth to save his life. Her sad plight is brought out in:

*apan dhan parke diye, diabaki beday mathay hat diye*

Giving her treasure to another, Daivaki suffers Krishna, was brought up Jasoda. Hence :

*kuntiye molo daibaki, naṃ padan jasodarani*

Daibaki suffered birth pangs and Jasoda gloats at her son's fame.

**Pralhad :** Though born among the demons he had great faith in God and shone because of his virtues, in short an exception:

*dvaityakuley pralhad*

A Pralhad among the demons

Harishchandra : King who had sacrificed his wife and son to repay debt and thus acquired heaven, and epitome of self sacrifice:

*harischandrer swargalabh*

Harishchandra's ascent to heaven.

**Savitri** : Known for her chastity. But if a women pretends to be like Savitri without being so, then she is mocked as,

*sati savitri*
Chaste Savitri

## III
## Historical Characters

The ordinary villagers were always curious not just about deities and mythological characters but also prominent figures from history, more particularly the history of their immediate surroundings. As elsewhere, here also the proverbs display a keen awareness of the characteristics of such personages.

**Mahipal** : A person whose virtues were not unknown even to the most humble. Thus:

*ghunte kath kudate genu, mahipaler geet penu*

Went to collect cowdung cake and sticks, heard songs in praise of Mahipal.

Sometimes proverb makers pitted eminent people against ordinary folk to highlight the former's qualities. Ramakrishna Roy was a famous raja of Natore (Bangladesh) and the proverb goes,

*kothay raja ramkrishna kothay bhaja jele*
Raja Ramakrishna and the fisherman Bhaja?

Or

*rani bhabani ar phool jeleni*

Rani Bhabani and Phool the fisherwoman?

Rani Bhabani was known for her religiosity and also for her generous nature.

**Chand Roy and Kedar Roy** : Two brother, famous zemindars of Bengal. There is a proverb to denote ungrateful people who took favours from one and praised the other:

*khay lay chand rayer, nan lay kedar rayer*

Takes from Chand Roy praises Kedar Roy

Among a God fearing people the general feeling was that he whom the Almight deprives cannot be helped by anybody.

Asaf-ud-Doulah, fourth Nawab of Oudh, was known for his large heart but proverb insists:

*yare day na khodatala, tarey day na asfuddoulah*

Him whom the Almighty denies, gets not from Asaf-ud-Doulah.

## IV

## Related to Society

Man is a social animal. Naturally whatever he sees in the world around him has found its place in the proverbs created by him. In this connection Sushil Kumar De's words deserve notice:

"All segments of social life have been portrayed in the proverbs, there is no subject that has not come within the ambit of humorous or mocking attention. People of all professions, farmers, milkmen, fishermen, barbers, goldsmiths, all castes, brahmins, kayasthas, vaidyas, all religions, Hindus and Muslims alike, zemindars their subjects, the rich and poor, the disabled, the thieves, ailments, relations between neighbours, all physical aspects of rural life-nothing has escaped the attention of the proverbs."[1]

Some examples of such proverbs:

*ude, nede, galay dadey, katha balbe e tin chhede*

Oriya, Muslim, keep them out of consideration

*bamun, badal, ban, dakshina pelei yan*

Brahmin, rains and flood, go after taking their due.

*kapale dirgha phonta, darshani chodda taka*

Long mark on forehead, fourteen rupees fee

(mocking reference to a Brahmin priest)

People belonging to the Vaishnava cult have also been mocked:

*mala ghoralei bairagi hay na*

Mere turning of prayer beads does not make a seeker of Truth

*telak katlei boshtom hay na*

marks on forehead do not a Vaishnava make

In a polygamous society the co-wife was always an object of suspicion:

*satiner hat saper chhon, chini dile tuley tho*

co-wife's hand is like a snake, even sweets she gives should be avoided.

Widowhood was always a painful experience, the widow had to observe many rites and was considered one who brought ill luck:

*akey rander bhat, tay musur dal*

Rice cooked by widow and then musur pulses

Widows were not supposed to eat the musur and the proverb hints at getting the undesired

Proverb on quacks:

*e paday yadi osudh khaoai, o paday mare ganda das*

Gives medicine here and kills many there.

Society had always been contemptuous of those show off:

*baire koncha lamba, bhitare astarambha*

Fancy dress, nothing inside

As for salaried people:

*kukurer ojor ache ta chakurer ojor nei*

Dogs have excuse not so the salaried man

The washerman cares not about the clothes he washes:

*yar phate tar phate, dhopar ki*

Washerman cares not whose clothes he damages.

The goldsmith is always out to steal when making ornaments:

*sekra mayer kaner sonao churi kare*

Goldsmith steals gold even from his mother's earrings.

The thief pays no need to good advice:

*chora na shoney dharmer kahini*

Thief has no time for religious discourse.

The drunkard has no sense. Hence:

*matal, dantal, shinge, biswas nei teene*

Drunkard, animal with teeth and horn, not to be trusted.

## V

## The Family

The family has always been important to the Bengali. To him the family does not mean the immediate family but includes all relations and even close friends. The proverbs on family members do not, however, reflect only love and affection but a deep understanding of human nature as well. For example the proverb on the Father:

*bape taka dileo nibi gune*

Count even the money that father gives.

The underlying meaning is, trust nobody.

It is the course different with the mother who is the central figure in the family, is loved and respected:

*mar gune poa, bhuin gune roa*

Mother's quality reflected in child, soil's in crop.

*maye marey, ma bolei kande*

Mother beats, baby cries calling out for mother.

*kisher masi, kisher pisi, kiser vrindavan*
*more gachhe phool phutechhe, ma bada dhan*
What aunts, what Vrindavan (holy place)
Flowers in dead tree, mother best treasure of all.

*ma nei yar, bifal janam tar*
Fruitless is life without mother

*asvather chhayai chhaya, mayer mayai maya*
Shade of the Asvatha tree and love of mother.

*mayer chapadey haad bhange na*
Mother's slap breaks no bones.

Brother-sister : *shashey kheye yeman jalke taan*
*temni bhaier bonke taan*
*chini kheye yeman jalke taan*
*temni boner bhaike taan*
As cucumber attracts water
so brother attracts sister
As sugar wants water
so sister wants brother.

**Paternal and Maternal aunts :** It appears there is love for the father's sister (*pisi*) and not so much for that of the mother's:

*baper bon pisi bhat kapade pushi*
*mayer bon masi, kaday phele thasi*
Father's sister, look after her
Mother's sister, trample her won mud.

The word 'masi' does not necessarily mean mother's sister, it applies to any elderly woman, just as any man can be addressed as 'dada' or elder brother. In general the 'masi' and object can also be of ridicule:

*masir gonf haley mama hoto*
If aunt grew moustache she would have been uncle.

Here something absurd or impossible has been referred to.

**Daughter :** The girl child was always a problem as she had to be given in marriage:

*dash putra sama kanya, yadi kanya patre padey*

Daughter like ten sons only if married off.

*meye manush parer bhagye khay*

Girls live off other's fortune.

The girl is always dependent on another.

*meye banchley jamair adar*

If daughter lives, son-in-law feted.

*meyer biye na kalipuja*

Daughter's marriage is like the Kali worship (an expensive festival).

**Wife :** In a family when girl comes as the son's wife, she has to face various forms of persecution from her in-laws, more so if the son is in love with her. Her mother-in-law very often shows her preference for her own daughter rather than the daughter-in-law. So the proverb:

*padmamukhi jhi amar parer ghare yay*

*ar unonmukhi bou esey batay paan khay*

My lotus faced daughter goes to another's home.

And oven -faced daughter-in-law eats betel leaves here.

*bou nay re bou nay, garal dakini*

*diner bela manusher chha, rat hole dakini*

Wife she is not, a poisonous witch

Human at day, witch at night.

*bouer chalan-feran Keman, na turki ghoda yeman*

Wife's manners are like that of a Turkish mare

*bouma khir railo khabe*

*na khao yamer badi yabe*

Daughter-in-law eat the dried milk

Don't eat, Yama will take you away (you will die).

*maer pete bhat nei, bouer chandrahar*

Mother does not get to eat, wife wears necklace

Proverb to humiliate a doting husband.

**Sister-in-law :** The sister-in-law and daughter-in-law seldom get along, with both trying to get the better of the other. Thus the daughter-in-law says,

*nanadini raibaghini dandiye achhe kalsapini*

There stands sister-in-law like a snake.

Sister-in-law retorts:

*bap kande ma kande achar bichar kheye*

*bhaier bou kande chokhe marich diye*

Father, mother weep uncontrollably

Brother's wife weeps putting chilli dust in her eyes

(Daughter-in-law sheds crocodile tears during times of sorrow).

*bhaier bouer baper badi dash dasi khate*

*sei garabe bou kebal buk phulie hante*

Many servants at brother's wife's place

So she just walks around proudly

Back to the daughter-in-law:

*bhalo katha mone podlo anchate anchate*

*thakurjhi ke niye gelo nachate nachate*

Oh yes, now I remember

Sister-in-law taken away across the river

She had seen her husband's sister being swept away by waves but had forgotten to say so, such was her indifference towards.

Son and Daughter : The son always preferred to the daughter and so:

*satjanme pap karli*

*maye janme tabe eli*

Sinned in your previous births

Born now as a daughter.

*chhele sikhuk likhapada*

*meye sikhuk rannabada*

Let son learn to read and write

Daughter to cook.

*chhelera hirer angti*

*meyera matir kalsi*

Sons are diamond rings

Daughters earthen pitchers.

*chhele biyole swargabas*

*meye biyole narakbas*

Give birth to son, heaven is yours

Birth to daughter and face hell.

The complex relationship between the mother-in-law and her son's wife is reflected in many other proverbs which bring out their inherent dislike for each other. Such as:

*eke bou nachni tay khemtar bajna*

The wife is always looking for fun and now dance music.

The mother-in-law is also always jealous of that son who pays a little more attention to his wife:

*ki karbe pute*
*kanbhanganir kachhe se ye nitya yay shute*

What can the boy do, every night he sleeps with her who poisons him.

On the other hand the wife wants a family without any female-in-law. So:

*ekla gharer ginni hobo*

*chabikathi jhuliye naite yaba*

I alone will be mistress in the house and will go to bathe with almirah keys dangling down my shoulder.

If the wife comes from a poor family, the mother-in-law loses no opportunity to rub it in:

*ghunte kundrunir meye pelo rajputtoor bar*

*muri murki dekhe bale-kon gachher phal*

Pauper's daughter gets prince as husband

Seeing puffed rice asks, fruits from which tree?

Relationship between the wife and the sister-in-law also finds expression in proverbs:

*bouer panja bhari, pa goda*

*bouke kichu bolo na dada*

Wife's hands are heavy, legs thick

Don't tell her anything brother dear.

And even when her brother punishes his wife, the sister mocks:

*data ki bou marey*?

*gamchhar badi mere tamasha kare*

Does brother beat his wife?

Pretends doing that but with a towel.

Proverbs on the wife's relations with the elder brother of her husband (*bhasur*) are marked by a sense of fun but not by any scorn or contempt.

*bhasur thakurer kole maag*

*sei bhabnay amar ghoom nei*

No woman in brother-in-law's laps

So worried, I cannot sleep.

Contempt, however, does creep in if the brother-in-law spends his days in idleness:

*niskarma bhasurer bachan mitha*

*nitya bose Khan chikan pitha*

Idle brother-in-law's words are sweet

Spends days eating crisp pies.

The son-in-law has a special position in the family but at the same time he is made to understand why he occupies that position. Like :

*meye banchle jamaier adar*

Son-in-law gets proper attention as long as daughter lives.

The need to pay proper attention to the son-in-law often also serves as an excuse for the rest of the family enjoying themselves. Thus :

*jamaier name maare hans*
*gushtisuddha khay maas*

Kills goose in the name of son-in-law

all eat the flesh

That son-in-law who lives with his in-laws is, however, an object of scorn:

*ghar jamai adha chakar, sarvaloke bale*

The resident son-in-law is half a servant, they all say.

*dur jamaier mathay chhati*
*ghar jamaier mukhe lathi*

Hold umbrella on the head of the visiting son-in-law, kick the resident son-in-law on the face.

Through these proverbs we get an idea of the nature of relationship that existed, and still does, within a Bengali family which in the past of course was much more extended than at present.

## VI
## The Human Body

From time immemorial man has been curious of his own body, he has sought to see the various parts in the light of his experience with the world at large and this is evident from the proverbs:

**Head :** *Chhotoloker katha, kachhoper matha*

Words who hides himself in fear, whose words have no value.

*mathar upar chhadi ghurano*

Waving the stick above the head

Supervising over others.

*matha nei tay matha byetha*

No head so what headache.

Worrying unnecessarily.

**Nose :** *naker chey naker dak beshi*

Snore is bigger than the nose

Part larger than the whole

*nak nei betir nather shakh*

No nose yet wants a nosering

Seeking something not needed.

**Mouth :** *parer mukhe jhaal khaoa*

Pasting spicy food through another's mouth

Believing in hearsay.

*mukhey madhu antarey bish*

Honey dripping from mouth, poison at heart

*mukh tuley chaoa*

Raising the face and looking.

This proverb means good times ahead as the Almighty has raised his face.

**Foot :** *chheler mata hat, pa budor mata katha*

Hand and foot like child, talks like the old.

**Finger:** *angul phule kalagachh hoa*

Finger swollen like a banana tree.

To become rich overnight, and develop arrogance

*soja angule ghee othe na*

Straight finger cannot bring out ghee (from a bottle)

Harsh means are needed when decency fails.

**Forehead:** The forehead is always associated with fate related statements and that is the case with proverbs also:

*mojurer kapaley chhenra chatai*

It is worker's fate to sleep on a torn mattress.

The poor have to do with inexpensive things.

*kapal gune gopal mele*

If fate is favourable divine help comes.

**Shoulders:** *parer ghadey banduk rekhe shikar kara*

Hunting by resting the gun on other's shouler.

Dependent on others for doing a job to avoid appleasant consequences.

**Teeth:** *dant thakte danter maryada bojheyna*

Not appreciating importance of teeth as long as they are there.

Not utilizing things properly at the proper time.

*yar pata tar noda*

*tari bhangi danter goda*

his grinding stone

use it to break his teeth

To harm a man with his own tools.

**Hair:** *chul niye ki petey shobo*

Will I use the hair to lie down on it?

An asset that does not really help.

**Feet:** *mathar gham paye phela*

Sweating from head to feet

Labouring hard.

*payeyer tala theke mati sorey yaoa*

Ground slipping from under the feet.

To lose all support.

**Back:** *petey khele pithey shay*
Back tolerates of stomach is full.
Hardship is tolerable in exchange of something.
*pithe kunj chand dekhar sadh*
Hunchback wants to see the moon
To try to achieve the impossible.

**Hand:** *ek haate tali baje na*
Can't clap with one hand
It takes two to tango.

## VII
## Manners, Habits

Many proverbs have been created on the basis of our behaviourism in our domestic life. These proverbs highlight the defects or faults in our behavioural pattern, particularly of women. A note of ridicule and scorn is noticeable in these proverbs:

*khatmatiye hante nari, katmatiye chay*

*mashek khanek bhitar tar sinthir sindur yay*

Walks the woman briskly, looks hard all around

Loses within a month the mark of marrige at hair's parting (becomes a widow).

Manly manners bring misfortune to a woman

*nachuntir laj nei, dekhuntir laj*

Dancer not ashamed, onlooker is.

Proverb speaks of a shameless woman.

*amar nam jamunadasi, parer khete bhalobasi*

Name is Jamuna Dasi, love to eat off others.

One who craves for others' things.

*bhat pay na bhatar chay*

Gets no food, wants husband

Making impossible demands.

*gram berani chutarani, tola jaley snan*

Loitering around the village, she bathes in water drawn for her.

Criticism of one given to excesses.

*samayer ek phonr, asamayer dash phonr*

Stitch in time saves nine.

*kajer moddhey dui, khai ar shui*

Only work is to eat and sleep.

Mother-in-law's snide remark about daughter-in-law.

*garaber garabini, ei paden nake nath ei paden kane*

Vain she is, now puts jewel on nose and now on the ear.

Another criticism of the daughter-in-law.

*bouti bhalo bate*
*tokna kheye batna bate*

The wife is good
Scolded, she grinds spices.

A good word for the daughter-in-law.

*yadi bale paker katha, tabe other mathar byatha*

Asked to cook, her head starts aching.

Criticism of the idle woman.

## VIII
## Related to Domestic Utensils

In our domestic life, a lot of utensils are needed for our daily life to run our family. People use these utensils to fulfill their daily necessities. As proverbs are closely related to our life, so many proverbs have been created in Bengal centring around the daily necessities of those utensils.

**Pitcher :** *shunya kalsir aoaj beshi*
Empty vessel sounds the most.

**Pot :** *yeman handi teman sara*
As is the pot so is the cover.
Made for each other.

**Bag :** *tholir bidal ber hoye pada*
Cat is out of the bag.

**Husking Pedal :** *dhenki swarge geleyo dhan bhane*
Even in heaven pedal husks paddy.
Habits die hard.

**Ladder :** *paka dhaney moi deoa*
Running ladder across ripe corn.
To spoil work that is completed.

**Knife :** *mukhe ram nam, bagale chhuri*
Talking the name of Ram with knife in armpit.
Saying good things while planning evil.

**Shoe :** *goru mere juto dan*
Killing a cow and then offering shoe.
Small compensation for grave misdeed.

**Sieve :** *chaluni bale chhunch ke, tor talay keno chhenda*
Sieve asks needle, why do you have a hole?
Pot calling the kettle black

**Quilt :** *chhenra kanthay shuiye lakh takar swapna*
Breaming of lakhs lying on a torn quit,
Having pipe dreams.

**Axe :** *nijer paye kudul mara*
Bringing axe down on one's own foot.
To cause harm to one's ownself.

## IX

## Related to Nature

Nature always plays its role for the human society to perplex them with the beauty of it.

Bengal is a land of rivers, vast open fields, snow capped mountains, the beauty of its nature finding expression in poetry, music, paintings, rhymes, riddles and of course in proverbs. The beauty of Bengal does not only attract litterateur, but also plays a major role in the creation of proverbs.

The proverbs relating to nature can be divided into two parts:

(a) Concerning plant life.

(b) Concerning the sky and planets.

Plant life : As in order parts of the country, nature has endowed Bengal with a wide range of trees, creepers, fruits, flowers and the proverbs are generally about those which are a part of daily life. Some examples :

**Mango :** Considered the king of fruits and the proverb runs:

*phaler madhye amro pha*
*jaler madhye gangajal*

Mango among fruits is what the Ganga is among rivers.

**Banana :** *kalapoda khao*
Eat burnt potatoes.

Such potatoes are an ingredient of the rites observed during funerals and the proverbs is a sort of curse.

**Jackfruits :** *kanthal kheye laglo atha*
*tel diye ghuchao letha*
jackfruit gum sticks to fingers
get rid of it with oil.

**Brinjal :** *panta bhate noon jote na*
*begun poday ghee*
No salt with the watered rice.
Ghee with roast brinjals.

Proverb ridicules the extravagance on the part of a poor man.

**Pulbul :** *bhay pay na sheikher beta*
*patal bhaja khay*
Fears not the sheikh's son
eats fried pulbul.

This also ridicules exrtravagance.

**Bottle-gourd :** een bought by Nanda Sau.
To be a fool and bring home useless things.

**Rose :** *golap bage kukur shonka*
An evil smelling tree in a rose garden.

**Lotus :** *goborey padmaphool*
Lotus in cowdung.

An exception in a dungheap.

**Champak :** *champa phooler gandhe, jamai ase anande*
Fragrance of champak brings son-in-law in joy.

As the bee is attracted by the flower's fragrance so is the son-in-law by the wife at her parents' home.

**Tree :** *bado gachhe jhad lage*
Storm hits the big tree.
The head of a family has to bear all troubles.
*gachhe tule moi tene neoa*

Dragging away the ladder after making somebody climb a tree.

To leave somebody high and dry.

Sky, Planets, etc

**Fire :** *benir agun laga haate*
Braid on fire, now hand affected
Problem acquiring serious proportion.

**Cloud and rain :** *megh na chaite jal*
Rain even before cloud has been sought.

Unexpected bounty.

**River :** *khar naditey char pade na*

Fast flowing river has no sand bed arising.

Speedy action fears no obstruction.

**Sea :** *samudre petichhi shajya, shsishire ki bhay*
Made the sea my bed, why fear the dew drop?
Immersed in troubled, small pinpricks do not matter.

**Mountain :** *akande yadi madhu pai*
*tabey keno parvate yai*
If the akanda flowers gives honey
Then why go to the mountain
Why go far if help is at hand.

**Moon :** *chand kapale dirgha phonta*
*mukh tar sarshe bata*
Forehead like the moon
Mustard paste in mouth.
Good looking person with a harsh tongue.
*chader kachhe jonaki poka*
Like the firefly to the moon

The small is not appreciated in the presence of the great.

**Sun, Rain :** *rod hay brishti hay*
*shial kukurer biye hay*
Sun and rain together
Fox and dog getting married.

Proverb on something absurd.

*boder bela helay yay*
*brishtir bela ghar chhay*
Idles away the sunny day
Thatches roof during rain

Wasting opportunity, then doing things at the wrong time.

## X
## Related to Agriculture

Farming being the principal occupation, it was natural that proverbs would be created around it: these are to be found particularly in the sayings of Khana, associated with which are the good and the bad. Some of the agriculture-related proverbs are following:

*Lanka punto gundo, begun budo*
Sow chillies small, brinjals big.
*narkeler goday mati*
*suparir goda kati*
Put earth at base of coconut tree.

Cut base of betelnut tree.
*char aal unchu, majkhane nichu*
High boundaries, low at middle
Proverb on how the land should be.
*pube hans pashchime bansh*
*uttare kala dakshine khola*
Duck pond in east, bamboo in the west
Banana north, south open
Proverb on what to grow in which direction.

## XI
## Related to Food

From time immemorial, Bengalis have been known for their love of cooking and eating. Their love of taking food can be found in Mukundaram Chakrabarty's 'Nidayar Sadhbhakhyan' which is a part of 'Chandimangal Kabya'. In 'Kalketur bhojonparba' of the same and in the poems of Iswar Gupta, this can also be found. It was thus only natural that the kitchen would enter the world of proverbs, once again the meaning often lying beyond the obvious:

**Chicken :** *ek murgi kabar jabai*
Killing the same chicken many times
Repeating, torturing over same issue repeatedly.

**Lemon :** *lebu chatkale tita hay*
Squeeze 100 much, the lemon turns bitter
Excessive pressure leads to unpleasantness.

**Banana :** *rath dekha kala becha*
Seeing chariots, selling bananas
Mixing business with pleasure.

**Ghee** (clarified butter) : *bhande nei ghee, thakthakale habe ki*
No ghee, pointless shaking the pot
No point in trying to hide emptiness inside.

**Buttermilk :** *dudher swad ghole matano*
Buttermilk to get the taste of milk
Trying to make do with a poor substitute.

**Curd :** *hate doi, pate doi, tobu bale koi, koi*
Curd on fingers, on plate, yet says where is it?
Never satisfied.

**Salt :** *noon ante panta phuray*
When salt arrives, the watered rice is finished.
Lengthy preparation defeats the purpose of the work.

## XII

## Related to Animals, Birds, Insects

From the ancient times, the life of mankind is closely associated with insects, birds, animals and the like. These are our friends and inseparable part of our existence. Hence, in some of our proverbs, the presence of animals, birds or insects are noteworthy.

**Cow :** *goru na biotei ghee*
Asking for ghee even before the cow has given hirth.
Hoping a step ahead.

**Dog :** *kukurer pete ghee shay na*
Dog's tummy can't accept ghee.
Everything is not for everybody.

**Cat :** *biraler bhagye shike chida*
Cat's good fortune that the hanging rope breaks and the food pot fall down.
Good luck.

**Tiger :** *yakhane bagher bhay, sekhane sandhya hay*
Everything descends where there is the fear of tiger.
Danger comes when it is most feared.

**Monkey :** *banarer galay muktar mala*
Pearl necklace around monkey's neck
Throwing pearls to the swine.

**Cuckoo :** *kokiler bou chhele dhartey jane na*
Mother cuckoo can't rear chicks.
Relates to inexperience. She cuckoo lays eggs in crow's nest.

**Parrot :** *labher dhan tia khay*
Parrot eats the paddy.
Income eaten away by expense.

**Ant :** *pipilikar pakha hay maraner tare*
Ant grows wings to die.
Ambition leads to collapse.

**Vulture :** *shakuner najar bhagader dike*
Vulture eyes dead animals
The mean always has eyes for the lowly.

**Fish:** *pani ghola kore machh dhara*
Fishing in troubled waters.

## XIII
## Musical Instruments

Musical instruments are being used in Bengal from the ancient times. The references of musical instruments are found from the literature of the Caryapad to the modern era. In a major part of the folk literature, especially in folk-songs, various types of musical instruments are needed. In Bengali Proverbs, there are examples of a lot of musical instruments. These instruments are known as folk-instruments. Here are examples of some proverbs based upon musical instruments :

**Drum :** *dhak thuiye chandipath*
Reading scriptures, putting drun aside
The lowly doing things beyond him.
*dharmer dhak apni baje*
Heavenly drum beats on its own
An evil deed cannot be kept concealed.
*hater majhe dhol peta*
To beat drum in the market place
To make public, to reveal a secret.

**Tom-tom :** *kai dai kansi bajai*
Eat and spend day beating tom-tom
Idling away time.

**Shehnai :** *sanair po dhara*
Beating to the shehnai's tune.
Blindly supporting or imitating.

## XIV

## Jewellery, Dress, Toilet items

Women loves to ornament themselves. The things which they use to ornament themselves are known as jewellery. To beautify themselves, women use various types of ornaments and toilet items. Therefore, in the proverbs, related to life, there are lac-dye, collyrium, and various types of jewellary. These toilet items have been used to create proverbs.

lac-dye : Nosering : *goda pay, alta, khyanda nake nath*
lac-dye on fat feet, nosering on snub nose
what is ugly cannot be decked up to look nice.
collyrium : *shudhu kajal porle hay na, chauni chai*
only collirium does not help, eyes must be good.
sandalwood paste : *kapal thuiye pachhay chandan*
putting sandalwood paste behind instead of forehead.
Wrong application.

**Sari :** *mayer galay dodi*
*bouke parai dhakai sari*
Rope around mother's neck
Sari from Dhaka for wife.
Ignoring mother for wife. A variation is,
nei ghar nei bari
bouke parai dhakai sari
No house to live in
Buy sari from Dhaka for wife.
Going out of way to please.

Also

*rajar badi chedi*
*dine satkhana shadi*

ugly palace maid
changes sari seven times a day.

Proverb to ridicule rich but bad looking woman's bid to look beautiful.

Women have always been attracted by ornaments and proverbs have been created keeping that in mind:

*goru, hal, beche gaday bouer galar har*

Sells cattle and plough to buy necklace for wife.

It is a mother-in-law's jibe at henpacked son.

*bhat pay na khete, sonar angti haate*

No food, gold ring on finger.

Men have also been ridiculed in such proverbs:

*nak nei tar atar gope*

No nose yet perfume on moustache

ghunte kudanirbeta elo dhuti chadar kinte

Cow dung picker's son buys dhoti and wrapper

*chul nei tar terikata*

No hair yet bothered about hairstyle.

## XV

## About Love

Proverbs are not used to ridicule only. In certain proverbs, tender feelings of love are expressed. However, in proverbs of love, with the expressions of emotion, sensitivity, and the like, jealousy is also expressed. Love is beyond any kind of bar regarding castes and religion. With this greatness of love, religious harmony and non-communalism were also expressed in some of the Bengali Proverbs.

*yar irsha nei se abar premik naki*

He who has no jealousy is no lover.

*dui deha, ek atma*

Two bodies, one soul.

*kadin pirit thake dhaka*

How long does love stay hidden?

*piriter nao pahade chale*

Boat of love climbs hills.

Proverb speaks of the dream world that love creates.

*yar sange yar maje mon*

*kiba hadi kiba dom*

When minds meet,

what do other things matter?

*pirit thakle tentu patay dujan shoa yay*

If there is love, two can sleep on a tamarind leaf.

## XVI

## About Place Names

Proverbs are also there about names of places. These bring out particular characteristics of the places, relating to the origin of the names and why these became well known.

(a) *shingh, shimla, kar*

*tin niye jajinagar*

Singh, Shimla, Kar

Three make up Jajinagar.

Jajinagar in Birbhum district was originally the home of people bearing surnames like Singh, Shimla and Kar.

(b) *pal, bhattacharya, khan*

*tin niye gram mankar*

Pal, Bhattacharya, Khan

Three make up Mankar

(c) *roy, banrujjeh, molla*

*tin niye khalla*

Roy, Banerjee, Molla

Three make up Khalla

Some villages got their names from the locals' occupation. Like:

(d) *ghentel, chetel phade*

*tin niye ulubere*

Ghentel ran the ferry service, chetel the inn and phade are middlemen or agents.

Particular castes and communities also marked some places:

(e) *bamun chandal musulman*
*tin niye pipulyan*

Brahmins, outcastes and Muslims marked the population of Pipulyan.

The people of Burdwan want to be seen in well dressed.

So :

(f ) *lamba koncha, kachhay tan*
*tabe janbe bardaman*

If the dhoti is well tied then it is Burdwan.

Shingarkon village near Burdwan is known for its culture and the proverb brings this out:

(g) *gan,bajna, sujan*
*tin niye singarkon*
Singing, music and good company
Three make up Singarkon

People of Manbhum are known for their addiction to betel leaves and the proverb goes:

(h) *mukhe pan, hate chun*
*tabe janbe manbhum*
Betel leaf in mouth and lime in hand
Know then this is Manbhum.

Kashi or Banaras is known for bullo, widows and mendicants:

(i) *shand, rand, sanyuasi*
bulls, widows, mendicants make Kasi
As for Calcutta

(j) *mithya kathar kiba keta*
*ajab shahar kolikata*
What ways of lying in this strange city Calcutta

There are two excellent proverbs on Kalighat.

(k) Tanti Rajput Bhat/Tin nie Kalighat. Kalighat consists of Tanti, Rajput, Bhat.

(l) Kalirakshar neiko pete Chandi porem Kalighat.

Though illeterate, yet recites Chandi at Kalighat.

Porverbs on the habits of food of Birbhum, the centre of Rarh, is found.

(m) Posto, tok, Kalaierdal Ei tin Birbhumer Chal.

(n) Kalapata, kather anti ei tin nie Baidyabati.

(o) Chor Chotta Haramjad Ei tin nie Murshidabad.

The proverbs describe a few characteristics of Birbhum, Baidyabati and Murshidabad.

People of Bengal are fond of different types of food; this reflects various provincial characteristics. In proverbs, social codes have been reflected. Like :

(A) Bandar Sabhakar Moder Ghora Ei nie Guptipara

(B) Tal babla chuncho Boncha Ei nie Murogacha.

(C) Dhan khur khal Ei tin nie Barishal.

In proverbs, different places of India, Kolkata and different areas of Kolkata are found. Even some districts of Bangladesh are also subjects of some proverbs. Besides sarcasm and ridicules, humour and wit also are reflected in a few proverbs.

## XVII

## Tales and Proverbs

There are some proverbs which carry folk-tales and parables with them. We have found a few proverbs of this types. Like:

*ghare ghare*

Within the family

A boy asked his mother who she was married to. When the mother hesitated, a neighbour said, "to your father". The boy replied, "Oh, within the family".[2]

*kangali merey kachhari garam*

Enliven the court by beating a beggar.

A landlord's courtiers were feeling out of sport as there was nothing by way of enjoyment in sight. Came a beggar and they decided to beat him up for fun. They did that and the court came to life.

*Makad malley dhokad hay*

Kill a spider and nothing happens.

A village boy asked the local pundit, what happens if a spider is killed. Seeing his opportunity, the pundit gave a long list of the rites that had to be performed to get rid of the sin. When the boy said it was his son who had killed the spider, the pundit replied, "you fool, don't you know that nothing happens if a Brahmin kills a spider".[3]

## XVIII

## Proverbs of Morals, Educational and Wisdom

A few proverbs which contain morals, educational stories and wisdom, are found in the domain of proverbs. In this class of proverbs, in the societies of Bengalis, teachings and knowledges, based upon villages of Bengal, are expressed in details. Like:

*tin matha yekhane*

*buddhi nibi sekhane*

Where three heads meet

Take counsel there

The message is : Take counself from an old man whose bent head is touching his knees—so three heads.

*ajey pa pare ga*

*mathay niye naite ya*

First feet, then body.

Take on head and go for bath

Lesson on how oil should be applied on the body before a bath.

*otha dhaner pathyi hay na*

Just harvested rice is not good for the sick.

*alo haoa bendho na*

*rog bhog sedho na*

Don't keep light, wind away

And invite diseases.

(a) *bedao yadi bhorer bela*

*thakbe na are roger jwala*

Early morning stroll

Keeps away ailments.

(b) Badyer madhye banshi

Roger modhye kashi

Flute is the best among musical instruments. Cough is the most dangerous disease among ailments.

## XIX

## Related to Popular Conclusions

In such proverbs it is noticed that the conclusion is firmly established with the help of examples and comparisons. Sometimes the examples tend to get confused with a touch of ridicule which makes it difficult to identify one from the other. The real purpose, however, is to establish the conclusion.

*ekhon bujhibe na youbaner bhare*

*takhon kandite habe ajjhor jhare*

Now you won't realise, being young

Later you will have to weep bitterly

*kisher mashi kisher pisi kiser vrindavan*

*mara gachhe phool phutechhe, ma bada dhan*

What aunts, what Vrindavan (place of pilgrimage)?

Mother is the biggest treasure of all.

*kather doshe karya nashta*

*bhikshay nashta mon*
Words spoil the work
Begging spoil the mind.

*ki majar shashur badi*
*yar peaysakodi achhe*
In-laws' place is great fun
For those who have money.

*joarer pani, narir youban*
High tide and woman's youth
Nothing is permanent.

*nijer chhele sonadhan*
*parer chhele dushman*
Own son is like gold
Other's son is a vandal

*parer sona diona kane*
*kede nebe hyanchka tane*
Don't use other's gold
Will snatch it away by force.

*purusher bal taka, narir bal shankha*
Money is man's strength, conchshell bangle woman's.
Such a bangle is a sign that her husband is alive.

*pate podlei khaoa hay na*
*rajay podleo rani hay na*
Food on plate doesn't indicate eating
To be with king does not make a queen.

*shankha, shadi, kesh, tine narir besh*
conchshell, bangle, sari and hair, three make a woman.

*sati nari gangajal*
*asat nari baddhajal*
Chaste woman gets the Ganga (holy river)

For others it is the pond water.

*yare dekhte nari tar chalan byenka*

Even the walk appears crooked of the person of dislike.

*phompra dhenkir shabda beshi*

Hollow husking pedal makes big noise.

Empty vessel sounds the most.

*ghar dekhe day ar bar dekhey day*

Gives seeing the house and the groom.

The daughter's father looks at the groom

The daughter's father looks at the home and the boy before giving his daughter in marriage.

## XX
## Related to Folk Journalism

In rural Bengal such proverbs played the role of mass media, conveying the message through word of mouth. From these proverbs, besides news and information, ridicule, sarcasm and force are also expressed with news. Some instances:

*guli, khili matichur*

*tin niye vishnupur*

Opium balls, rolled betel leaf and motichur (a sweet)

Three make up Vishnupur.

*ganja, tari, prabanchana*

*tin niye sarsuna*

Indian hemp, toddy, cheating

All three in Sarsuna (South of Calcutta).

*kagaj, kalam, kali*

*tin niye bali*

Paper, pen, ink

These make Bally

Proverb spreads the information that paper, pen and ink were made in Bally, west of Calcutta.

*ambikanagar gechhe gane*

*khatra gechhe dane*

*raipur gechhe bane*

Music saw the end of Ambikanagar

Charity saw the end of Khatra

Floods that of Raipur.

All these places were in Bankura district. Proverbs inform the ruler of Ambikanagar spent his fortune on music, that of Khatra on Charity and floods took care of Raipur, which was destroyed as a result of the flood in the river, Kangsabati.

## XXI
## Miscellaneous

So far we have discussed the Bengali proverb under various headings. Folk-literature deals with multi dimensional aspects of life and so it cannot be framed in a specific paradigm. In case of proverbs, it suits mostly in the lives of Bengalis, to whom these proverbs play a major role. There are many associated with aspects of life which do not attract sufficient attention, particularly those of a woman's life. In the ups and downs of the livelihood of people, we do not give importance to those subjects, which are expressed in proverbs. As the construction of proverbs have originated in the alleys of our livelihood, so in the mirrors of proverbs, these are reflected. We shall now take a look at proverb related to such aspects:

**Torture of Women:**

*yata yai karo na keno*

*purusher nichey thakbe yeno*

Do what you will

Under men shall you live.

*gorur matan boukey na marle*
*hay na sidhe konokale*
If like cows wives are not beaten
Behave properly they never will.

*besh hayechhe bamun thakur*
*tomar katha mani*
*baro bachare bia hayeche*
*swmi bole na jani*
Brahmin priest, as ordered by you
Got married at age twelve
Know not what husband is.

This proverb relates to child marriage.

Also:

*bibi yakhan bado habe*
*mian takhan kabar pabe*
When wife grows old
Husband is in the grave.

**Male and Female Child:**

*Chhele shikhbe lekhapada*
*meye shikhbe ranna kara*
boy will learn to read and write
girl will learn to cook.

*putra sampad meye apad*
Boy an asset, girl a liability.

*chhele biyole swargabas*
*meye biyole narakbas*
Heavenly if boy is born
Hell if child is girl.

**Women's Education:**

*meye yato pash debe*

*mathay tata chare basbe*
More educated the girl
More she will dominate.

*nari shiksha na hole*
*samay pichhoy pale pale*
Without women's education
Time goes back every moment.

*Shiksha chokh photay*
*meye keno thakbe pichhiye tay*
Education opens the eyes
Why should girls remain backward?

**Old Ideas of Women:**

*purusher galay mala diye*
*nari thakbe khate shue*
Putting garland round man's neck
Woman will lie down on bed.

*bhatar anbe upay kore*
*mag thakbe ghare ghare*
Husband will earn
Woman will stay indoors.

**Of Fallen Women:**

*khete pele shute chay*
*shue shue gaina chay*
Given food wants a bed
Lying down wants jewellery.

*dhyamna magir dhyamna mon*
*parpurushke kare apanjan*
Hussy with a warped mind
Makes strangers her own.

**Dowry System:**

*pon chhara, biye*

*ki habe se meye niye*

Marriage without dowry

Why bring such a girl home.

*koner ma kande*

*takar puntuli bande*

Bride's mother weeps

And ties money in bundles.

*handi kinbe bajiye*

*kone anbe sajiye*

Buy pitcher after sounding it

Bring bride after she is well decked.

**Concerning Widows:**

*sabar kapale sindoor dekhe*

*bidhabara mare dukhe*

Seeing vermillion marks (sign of marriage) on other's forehads

Widows weep in sorrow.

*bidhabar jeevan*

*prattashay sarvakshan*

Widow's life

One of constant expectation.

**Drinking and Smoking:**

*tele tamake pittanash*

*yadi karo baromas*

oil, tobacco harmful

If taken twelve months.

*dinek madya pan kore*

*ek hapta matha dhare*

Drink one day
Headache for a week.
*mejaj ane dhumpane*
smoking brings good mood.

**Working People:**

*khete khaoa yader barat*
*katbe na tader dukher rat*
Those fated to toil for food
Will see no end to nights of sorrow.
*malikke ye sukhe rakhe*
*tar baratey dukh na thake*
He who keeps owner happy
knows no sorrow.

The proverb was of course created at a time when workers had not become conscious of their rights.

*gariber sab barat*
*bancha sei iswarer hat*
For the poor there is only fate
Their lives depend on the Almighty.

**Old Age :**

*budo bayase dhadipana*
*na hay sukh kebal yatana*
Behaving like young in old age
Brings no pleasure only pain.
*budo haile buddhisuddhi lop pay*
Old age sees senses disappearing.
*bayase aneker matha sada hay*
*swavab sada hay na*
With age many heads turn white
But not nature. (Nature does not change.)

**Physical Handicap:**

*andher kiba din kiba rat*

Blind has neither day nor night.

Proverb means helpless man has no choice.

*Iyangra hay yata chyangda chhonda*

Lame become the flippant youth.

More a warning against flippancy than anything else.

**Health Related:**

*dakshin duari gharer raja*

*purba duari tar praja*

South open is king of rooms

East facing is his subject.

*age tita pachhe mitha*

Bitter first, sweet later.

Typical Bengali way of eating.

Hope and Frustration:

*ashay param sukh*

*nirashay param dukh*

**Hope brings happiness:**

Frustration, sadness.

*pinra pete karnu thain*

*bada bhate parlo chhai*

Made arrangement for eating

Drops ash on the rice.

Hopès getting dashed.

**To Ridicule:**

*hati ghoda gelo tal*

*bheda bale kata jal*

Horses and elephants go under

sheep wants to test the depth.

Somewhat close to, Fools rush where angels fear to tread.

*kunde ghare bas*

*khat palanker ash*

Living in a cottage

Dreaming of a royal bed.

**Fate Related:**

*kapaler likhan*

*na yay khandan*

What is written

Cannot be undone.

*abhaga yay bange*

*kapal yay sange*

Hapless carries his fate with him.

**Justice Denied:**

*Chor khay churi kari bosi*

*niraparadher galay roshi*

Thief enjoys his stolen property

Innocent is hanged.

**Application of Force:**

*bhaluk ki nachte chay*

*nake dodi diye nachay*

Bear does not want to dance

Is forced to with rope round the nose.

*parechhi mughaler hate*

*khana khete habe sathe*

Caught by a Mughal

Forced to eat with him.

To bow down to the mighty, the Mughal being a representative of the Latter whom the Hindus, despite reservation, had to obey.

**In a Dilemma:**

*hageo na*

*patho chhade na*

Neither does it shit

Nor does it give way.

**Showing of:**

*baire baire nam phate*

*gharer maia kainda mare*

Outside he enjoys fame

At home daughter dies weeping.

*bahir badi lanthan*

*bhithar badi thanthan*

Lantern in the front room

Inside nothing.

**Hypocrisy:**

*mukhe khub mithe*

*neem nishinda pete*

Tongue is sweet

Bitter inside.

*dine kare sadhugiri*

*churi sararat*

Holy man during the day

Thief at night.

**Enmity:**

*gachher shatru lata*

*manusher shatru katha*

Tree's enemy is a creeper

Man's enemy is words.

**Selfishness:**

*apan charkay tel dao*

*Oil your own machine*

*Chacha apan jan bancha*

Uncle, save yourself.

Without bothering about others.

*ap bhala jagat bhala*

If I am alright, so is the world.

*apni banchle baper nam*

First me then the family.

**Contradiction :**

*dushtu gorur chey shunya goal bhalo*

Empty cowshd better than a naughty cow

*ye goru dudh day tar lathio bhalo*

The milch cow's kick is alright.

**Crookedness :**

*parer ghade bandook rekhe shikar kara*

Shooting with gun on another's shoulder.

*parer mathay kanthal bhanga*

Cracking open jackfruit on another's head

Living at the cost of others.

*dhori machh na chhuin pani*

Fishing without touching water

Reaping benefits without getting involved.

**Opportunism :**

*kajer belay kaji, kaj phurule paji*

Using one and forgetting him once the purpose is served.

Relating to Judges:

*hakim nade to hukum nade na*

Judge may waver but not the judgement.

*loghu pape guru danda*

Light crime, harsh punishment.

**On Doing Things:**

*adhik sanyasi te gajan nashta*

Too many holymen spoil the ritual song

Too many cooks spoil the broth.

*bämun gelo ghar, langal tule dhar*

Brahmin has gone home, shoulder the plough.

To avoid work, to be a shirker.

**Superstition :**

jhade bak mare fakirer keramati bare

Crane dies in storm, *fakir* claims credit.

Some proverbs were born out of feudal oppression:

*jor yar muluk tar*

He who is mighty owns the land.

*rajay rajay yuddha hay, ulukhagdar pran yay*

Kings fight, the grass died.

The 'grass' is the ordinary man.

The tendency to declare oneself leader whether others agree or not finds expression in:

*ganye mane na, apni modol*

Villagers don't accept but he calls himself a leader.

## References

De, Sushil Kumar: Banglar Probad, 1401, p. 46.

Bhattacharya, Asutosh: Banglar Lok Sahitya, 6th Vol., 1972, p. 601.

Sengupta Pallab: Lok Sanskritir Seemana O Swarup, 2002, p. 159.

# 3

# Bengali Society in Proverbs

"One of the main sectors of religious rituals is society. Where a few men and women live, depending on each other, society takes shape there. Every society has a few codes of conduct. Codes of conduct have two forms—written and non-written. The written form consists of rules and regulations for the benefits of most of the people having affirmative decisions of them. The unwritten facts consists of rules and forms of conducts which take shape through the dialogues among people"[1]—This comment is of Sahityaratna Harekrishna Mukhopadhyay. What he is talking about can be found in the literary scenario of folk literature and culture. Proverbs of Bengal are like the mirrors of the village-based life. Various subjects of Bengali society are reflected here. It is not that in all proverbs, the social-scenario of a specific time is found. However, in proverbs, social scenario of different times are found. Thus, proverbs reflect socio-economic history, lifelihood, rituals, beliefs, and several experiences of a society. Without cultivating proverbs, the study of the society of Bengal is impossible.

It will perhaps not be an exaggeration to suggest that since proverbs reflect various aspects of life in rural society and these considered a vehicle of people's culture, it is through the proverbs that we come to have a fair idea of ways of life, customs, superstitions, and the varied experiences of the past.

Women play a large role in proverbs, they are the creators of most. There was nothing unusual about this as Bengali society evolved around the home and in the home the woman occupied centre stage. And, as Rabindranath Tagore said, "It is the family which provides the foundation of any civilisation, without it people would have got scattered and not come together to build, the family held them together and the first task in this was performed by women".[2] Not that men do not feature in the proverbs but they feature in the way they are perceived by women. Woman is critical of man but that is not the whole picture, she is also often self-critical and taken together her psychology is admirably mirrored in the proverbs.

Talking of Bengali society, social scientist Benoy Ghosh wrote: "In West Bengal, different castes and tribes occupy such distinct social strata that it is not possible to have a single rural culture, that culture has many contradictory trends and elements mixed in it".[3] This is revealed in the proverbs:

*parechhi yavaner hate*
*khana khete habe sathe*

Am in the grips of the Muslim
Will have to dine with him.

*dom bagdi horel jat*
*posh na mane adhek rat*

The dom, bagdi and such untouchables
Cannot be tamed.

*Chashar hate shalgram maran*
The *salgram* dies in the hands of the peasant.

Marriages were very important in the family and not free from complications imposed by social customs like the dowry. The custom, though ruinous for the daughter's parents, had to be obeyed and so:

*Kodi bina shashurbadi yaoa yay na*
Cannot go to in-law's place without money.

And if the girl was dark complexioned, the dowry demanded became even more:

*kalo meye ki thakbe ghare*
*sab bikobe bazar dare*

Dark girls will not remain at home
All will be sold at market rates.

Not just dowry, there were also the evils of polygamy and child marriage. Society looked down on girls who had not been married before they entered thirteens and thus the proverb:

*ye meyer biye hay na*
*se toh samajer phelna*

The unmarried girl
Is a waste.

As for polygamy:

*bhage parechhe ekta chheler janya panchta meye*
*tai yata khushi meyeke kado tumi biye*

Every boy has five girls as his share
So marry as many as you want.

Marriages were fixed strictly by parents, the girl had no say. So:

*baba ma yake bolbe biye korte*
*tari galay habe kanyake mala dite*

Whom the parents order
The girl will have to marry.

The desperation to get daughters married off, by both Hindus and Muslims, often led to disastrous consequences:

*bibi yakhan bado habe*
*mian takhan kabar pabe*

When wife comes of age
Husband is in the grave.

More on polygamy:

*ek magke bhat day na*

*arek mager sadh*

Can't feed one wife

Wants another.

*ek barer mag hela-phela*

*dojbarer mag galay mala*

First wife ignored

Second wife garlanded.

Bengali society had for long believed marriage was for getting sons - *putrarthe kriyate bharya* - as it was the son who would "deliver" the parents from all evils. As we have seen in the earlier chapter this led to girl children being ignored and even considered a curse as reflected in the concerned proverbs. A few more of such proverbs:

*putra bale bamsa bade*
*kanya yabe parer ghare*

Son helps continuation of clan
Daughter will go to another's home.

*Chhele holo hirer tukro*
*meye holo khudkundo*

Son is a piece of diamond

Daughter a bit of broken grain.

It was natural that a male dominated society would seek to constantly undermine the position of women but strangely the latter, as creator of most of these proverbs, also seemed to accept this. Thus it was thought pointless to educate girls,

*meyera yatai likhapada shikhhuk*
*khunti toh narbe*

How much women may study
They will only cook.

And it was even believed that education will bring widowhood:

*likhapara shikhle*
*bidhava habe akale*

Learn to read and write
And be an untimely widow.

The widow of course had no role to play in society:

*purush karbe ya khushi tai*
*bidhavar tate nak galate nai*

Man will do whatever he pleases
Widow should not poke her nose in his affairs.

Widows of course could burn themselves on their husbands' funeral pyres:

*patir marane satir maran*

Husband's death meant the chaste woman's death.

In the days when polygamy was rife, the woman's main curse was the co-wife and this got reflected in the proverbs they created:

*yamake bhatar dite pari*
*satinke tobu dite nari*

Can hand over husband to yama
But not to co-wife.

*satiner hat saper chon*
*chini dile tule tho*

co-wife's hand is like snake's bite
If she gives sugar keep it away.

*sab kichhuk bhag deoa yay*
*swamir bhag na chhada yay*

Can share everything
Not the husband.

*eka chilam gharer majhe mathar thakur*
*satin elo aastakurer holam kukur*

When I was the only one I was the goddess
Came co-wife, I became a dog at the garbage heap.

The son of the co-wife is also treated similarly:

*satiner poer hat diye sap dharano*
Getting co-wife's son to catch a snake.

He on his part says:

*satmar mukh nada*
*sabar upar yena khanda*

Foster mother's words
Come down as a sword on all.

A male dominated society insisted on chastity at all costs and ordained that a chaste woman was she who blindly obeyed her husband. Hence:

*patir paye thake*
*tare bale sati*

Lies at the feet of husband
That is the chaste woman.

As for other women:

*yatai karo shivasadhana*
*kalankini nam yabe na*

Worship Siva for all you can

Will still be known as a fallen woman.

*pudbe nari, udbe chhai*
*tabu na tar kalanka yay*

Woman will burn
ashes will fly but will still be known as unchaste.

Fun has also been made of those pretending to be chaste:

*machh chhedichhi, mamsa chhedechhi dharme diyechhi mon*
*briddha beshya tapaswini yachhe vrindavan*

Given up fish, meat, taken to religion
Old harlot turned religious going to Vrindavan
(Vrindavan: associated with Lord Krishna.)

A caste divided society had assigned specific tasks to each caste. The *tilis* were traders, *tambulis* betel leaf cultivators, *malakars* dealt with flowers, the *gop* with cattle, *napit* was the barber etc. These were hackward castes but had the right to have priests from within their communities, as did the *kolu* (oil merchants) *syakra* (jeweller), *shundi* (wine merchants) and such others. But whatever the job division, in keeping with caste, might have been, it was those who did manual labour who really kept society going and spent lives of hardship. Their sorrow, their toil, is also the subject matter of proverbs:

*mukhe katha nay*
*kajey katha kay*

speak no words
work speaks for them.

*abhaga yedike chay*
*sagar sukhay yay*

Wherever the hapless looks
Finds the sea has dried up.

*garibke khete khete morte habe*
*kon bhaya ar ki karbe*

Poor will have to die toiling
Who can do anything about it.

*majurke lathi*
*hujurke salam*

Kick the worker
salute the master.

Fun has also been made of the upper castes. Even the brahmin who earns his livelihood by tending to spiritual needs of disciples has not been spared:

*kalir aksar naiko pete, chandi paden kalighate*
No education in him yet reads the scriptures.

About the shrewd kayastha:
*kak dhurta, kayet dhurta*

Crow is shrewd, so is the kayastha.

In a feudal system, the zamindar or landlord was known, and hated, for his oppressive ways. So:

*sap, shala, jamidar, tin nay apnar*

Snake, brother-in-law and zamindar can never be your own.

As for his iron rule:

*baghe, gorute ek ghate jal khay*
Tiger and cow drink from the same spot.

*jor yar muluk tar*
He who is mighty rules the land.

The physician or vaidya has always been considered an extortionists:

*vaidyar bodi, chhunle kodi*
Physician's tablet, touch and spent money.

*vaidya taka chhada kichhu kare na*
Physician does nothing without money.

As for his powers to cure:

*e paday yadi ousudh kaoai, o paday mare ganda dash*

(His) medicine here kills many there.

A man's means of living determined his place in society and any change caused confusion and trouble:

*napit hailo kaviraj, kshouri kare ke*

Barber has become doctor, who will shave?

*kheto tanti tant bune*
*kal holo tar enre goru kine*
Weaver was happy weaving
Met his end buying a barren cow.

Experience caused the proverb maker to make fun of some professions. The milkman for instance:

*gai gayla bhab thakle*
*ek ser dudh ek hantu jale*

If cow and milkman are friends
Seer of milk in knee high water.

An object of mistrust also is the jeweller:

*syakra nijer maer kaner sona churi kare*

Jeweller steals gold from even his mother's earring.

In rural Bengal the monks of the Vaishnav community, who depended on alms for their livelihood, were often ridiculed and looked down upon. Thus:

*sadhe ki bairagi nache, bhater thala hater kachhe*

No wonder the Vairagi dances, the plate of rice is within his reach.

*mala ghoralei bairagi hay na*

Prayer beads alone do not a monk make.

*telak katlei bosatom hay na*

Mere marks of piety (on forehead) do not a Vaishnav make.

Proverbs on peasants and fishermen highlight their sorry plight:

*chasha mare se bhalo, parer kaste yena na haray*

Peasant dies, no problem, should not lose the borrowed sickle.

*chashar duksha egaro mas*

Peasant suffers eleven months.

*jeler parane tena, panjarir kane sona*

Fisherman wears loincloth, fish trader has gold on his ears.

As for the blacksmith:

*kamar budo hole bherendar gachhe sar*

Old blacksmith is good for fertilising trees.

The salaried person is bound by rules and discipline:

*chhoto kukurer ojar achhe, chakurer ojar nai*

Even the little dog can give excuses, not the salaried person.

Lawyers were considered people who complicated matters in their own interest. So in the case of a dispute with somebody,

*ukil pathabe na, nije yabe*

Don't send lawyer, go yourself.

As for the Marriage maker:

*Samje ghatak jati bada chatur*

In society the marriage makers are very clever.

And the drunkard is not to be trusted:

*Metal, dantal, shinge, biswas nei teene*

Trust not the drunkard, horned animal and the bull.

There is no point in preaching morals to the thief:

*chora na shone dharmer kahini*

Thief does not listen to scriptures.

*Chor khonje andhar rat*

Thief looks for the dark night.

It takes all kinds to make up a society and proverbs draw attention to their characteristics to arrive at a general conclusion. Like:

*kuloy shue tuloe dudh khan*

Lying in a winnow sucks milk from cotton threads.

An unusually fussy comfort loving man.

*nachte neme ghomta tana*

Covering the face with sari end while dancing.

A person pretending to be shy.

*bhitare phank yata yar, baire dhaka tata tar*

Deeper the hollow inside, stronger the outside cover.

Similar to, Empty vessel sounds the most.

*alpa vidya bhayankari*

Little learning is a dangerous thing.

There are many proverbs on love:

*chokhe chokhe yatakshan pran prode tatakshan*

As long as eyes meet, the heart burns.

*Piriter petnio bhalo*

Love makes even the ugly beautiful.

*yar sange bhav, tar mukh dekhao lav*

Even a look at the loved one's face is enough.

Some proverbs impart lessons:

*mala jap michhe mon hay pichhe*

Turning prayer beads meaningless if mind is elsewhere.

Farmers are not supposed to touch the haystack on Mondays and Wednesdays for that brings ill luck:

*som budhe deo na hat*
*dhar kore kheo bhat*

Touch not on Monday, Wednesday
Get rice (if needed) on loan.

*kachchhap, ajatra*

See tortoise, journey will be spoilt.

Society's cruelty is brought out in a proverb like,

*atkudar mukh dekhli din yay upabase*

Seen the barren woman will starve the day.

Marriage is a sacred institution and involves the bride going seven times round the bridegroom to make the bond permanent. Proverb says,

*Satpaker biye chodda pake khole na*

Marriage of seven rounds won't come apart even with fourteen rounds.

As marriages, and other such occasions, relatives crowd the house but are rarely of any help. The mistress of the house is thus happy when the exception arrives:

*emon kutum kotha pai*
*gadakhan thuey lejakhan khay*

where is that relative who sets aside
the best fish and eats the tail.

Guests, however, are not unwelcome:

*yekhane gerasther basa*
*sekhane atithir asha*

where there is a householder
there the guest has hope.

but if the guest outstays his welcome:
*machh ar atithi dudin pare bish*

Fish and guests turn poisonous with time. Some guests are special, like the *behai* or father of the daughter-in-law or son-in-law:

*eso behai baso behai*
*dui behai tamak khai*
*tomar meye amar chhele*
*ghar karchhe manda nay*

Come behai come and sit
Have a smoke with me
Your daughter, my son
Are living happily together.

The great belief in fate finds expression in:

*adrishter phal ke khandabe bala*

What fate has in store cannot be undone.

Proverbs warn against taking loan:

*karja kare ye kashta pay se*

He who takes loans suffers

*karja kare ghee khay chirakal kashta pay*

Takes loan for ghee (a luxury item) and suffers.

In the olden days *kodi* was the medium of exchange. He who had *kodi* ruled the world, as they do today also:

*yar kodi tar jay*

Has money, is the winner.

There was a time when poor low castes had to give free labour and the resentment against it is clear in:

*arajye bamun begar*

In a bad world even the Brahmin gives free labour.

In an age when family planning was not practised, the warning came from the proverb maker:

*adhik santan yar, ashesh durgati tar*

Who has many children, faces endless suffering.

Another one against drinking:

*ye ghare madhy dhoke*
*lajja palay se ghar theke*

Home where liquor enters
Has shame running out of it.

*dine madya pan kare*
*ek hapta matha dhare*

Drink during day
Headache for a week.

Glimpses of social history and popular anecdotes are found in some of the proverbs:

*lage taka debe gouri sen*

Need money Gouri Sen will provide it.

Reference is to a proverbially rich and generous man.

*kalighater kangali*

Beggars of Kalighat

*bheto bangali*

Rice eating Bengali

Reference to the supposedly indolent nature of Bengalis.

*Pashchime sadhu, pube babu*

Holymen in the West, baboos in the East.

Another reference to the Bengali character. Also,

*gharmukho bangali, ranmukho sepai*

Bengali heads for home, the sepoy for war.

In a caste divided society, some among the upper castes enjoyed additional status:

*Ghosh, bose, mitra, kuler adhikari*
*Balir dutta yan yan gadagodi*

Ghosh, Bose, Mitra enjoy special status
Dutta of Bally finds place nowhere.

As for the characteristics of different upper castes:

*Ghosh bamsa bada bamsa, bose bamsa data*
*mitra ati kutil, dutta haramjada*

*Ghosh is noble, bose charitable*
Mitra is crooked, Dutta a scoundrel;

The observance of rites and rituals (brata) took up the daily lives of Bengali women and so almanao had to be constantly consulted. The dates of some were, however, too well known to be checked. Like ambubachi on the seventh day of the month of ashadh:

*satoi ashadh ambubachi*
*nei kono tar panji punthi*

Ambubachi on Seventh Assadh
No almanac needed to know that.

As already stated most such proverbs were women centric. Some more illustrations:

*narir bal, chokher jal*
Women's strength is her tears.

*Garaber garabini, ei paren nake nath, ei paren kane*
Proud woman, now a nosering now an earring.

*joan dekhe dharlam bhatar, shoe hage rakta*
Got a strong husband, he also shits blood.

*marader jide badshah, maiar jide beshya*
Man's determination will make him king, woman's prostitute.

*Yatai karo shivsadhana, kalankini nam yabe na*
No matter how much you pray, your unchaste tag won't go.

*yubakale ranga kare, bridhhakale sati*
After fun in youth turning chaste in old age.

Discussing on the reflection of society in proverbs, a specialist on this subject has once said, "the birthplace of proverbs has been originated from the urge of expression of feelings of our innermost mind. Proverbs include the vast canvas of our livelihood, experiences, morals, theories, humours, happiness, sorrow, hope, despair, love, jealousy, hatred, praises, fortune and misfortune, agriculture, industry, business, cloud and rain, draught and flood, and everything else, which are closely related to our society. Therefore, from family, religion, castes to various fields of works, hierarchy has also been included in proverbs."[4]

Therefore, proverbs exfoliate the human-psychology in a large domain. Either in a tone of ridicule or in a form of humour, proverbs represent a kind of codes of society and everyday lifelihood. From the origin of the development of Bengali soul, proverbs have been created to cannonize Bengali soceity. To know every aspect of Bengali society, we should cultivate its proverbs.

## References

1. Mukhopadhyay, Harekrishna, Gourbangasanskriti, edited by Biswanath Ray, second edition, 1406, p. 65.
2. Tagore Rabindranath : Nari, Kalantar. Rabindra Rachanabati (edition, published by West Bengal Government), thirteenth part, 1990, p. 673.
3. Ghosh, Binoy : Sanskritir Samajik Duratya, Ekaler Prabandha Sanchayan, 1992, pp. 220-221.
4. Edited by Daschoudhari, Gopal & Sen, Priyaranjan, Prabad Prabachan, 1367, p. 2.

# 4

# Proverbs As Means of Protest

Protest is a means of expressing the will to resist. This expression is the outcome of some psychological phenomenon. When the baby cries, throwing around its small hands and feet, it is an instinctive protest. The blind and the dumb protest in their own ways. The banners at political meets and processions, the clenched fists, are all symbols of protest. Since the very early times man has protested against what he sees as injustice and that protest has found expression in his creation, his music, his poetry.

Protest is age old because so has been oppression. The class division that Marx spoke about saw to a handful piling up wealth, depriving the masses who naturally had to rise in protest. Here we are focussing on Bengali proverbs. From the ancient times, literature is the means to reflect protests against the power structure. Oppression is a kind of social disease. This disease has its vast range which incorporates social, economic, religious, and psychological aspects.

The economic oppression has also had its social manifestations and over the ages women and children have been the main victime of this. The proverb having been born out of man's experience in society reflected such oppression and the protest against it. This is what makes these apparently simple statements but carrying deeper meanings, so important to the social scientists. They find in the proverbs many forms of injustice, deprivation and pain, contradiction, resentment as also anger and scorn.

In domestic life the principal contradiction has always been between the mother-in-law and the daughter-in-law.

The latter sees the former as a tyrant and dreams of the day when she will no longer have her around:

*Ekla ghare ginni haba*

Will be the mistress of the house.

or

*shashuri nei, hanad nei, kar ba kori dar*

*age khai panta bhat, sheshe lepi ghar*

No mother-in-law, sister-in-law, whom do I fear

Will first have my meal then clean the room.

As for the mother-in-law she sees her son's wife as an irritant, like itches during summer—*garam kale ghamachi.*

Not that the mother-in-law has no case in her favour. After a time she feels lonely and so:

*beta biyolam, boure dilam*

*meye biyolam, jamalike dilam*

*apni holam bandi, pa chhadieh kandi*

Had son, gave to daughter-in-law

Had daughter, gave to son-in-law

Now a slave, I can only weep.

In the above proverb the mother calls herself a slave but actually that is what she wants her daughter-in-law to be:

*hater khadu beche ami kine anlam bandi*

*se holo ginni ar ami base randhi*

sold bangle to buy a slave

now she is mistress and I cook.

Such attitude of the mother-in-law perhaps can be explained by the fact that in her younger days, as a newly wed bride, she too had faced similar treatment. Thus it has been a continuing process, a never ending malaise of Bengali social life and of lives in other communities also. Protest against this is inherent in the reflection of the malaise in the proverbs.

The wife's problems are compounded when she also has to put up with the neglect of the husband whom she cherishes most. She protests:

*yar janya banabasi, sei day galay fansi*

Hangs me the man for whom I am in exile.

As for this tortures on her:

*yar janya buk phate, se amare kate*

Cuts me he for whom my heart breaks.

And she is full of rebuke:

*Kaje kunre khete dede, bachane mare tere phunre*

Idler, eats a lot, conquers all with his words.

*bhat day na bhatare, bhat day gatore*

Husband feeds me not, my labours do.

*Parechhi dajjaler hate, janjal jaday dine rate*

Am in the grips of this bully, have to handle garbage day and night.

To the wife the husband cannot be made to understand anything, he is like the *dhenki* which only knows how to husk paddy.

It is not only the wife who protests but the mother also who sees her son as always siding with her daughter-in-law:

*ma mare puter lagi*

*put mare bouer lagi*

Mother is all for her son
Son is all for wife.

Realizing this she changes her stance in her own interest:

*boure sebile putere pai*

Serving daughter-in-law, I get my son.

The wife's anger gradually takes in the world around her and she lambasts the hypocrisy she sees there:

*kukur mare handi phele na*

Beats the dog, does not throw pot away.

Despite all talks of cleanliness the pot in which the dog put its mouth is not thrown away.

*gharer ma bhat pay na, parer maer janya kanna*
Does not feed own mother, weeps for another's.

*goru mere juto dan*
Kills cow then gifts shoes.

*choonch gadte pare na,*
*bonduk bayna nay*

Can't make a needle,
takes orders for a gun.

There are proverbs protesting against showing off, trickery, shamelessness and against injustice:

*ghar nei bhat, jamidari that*
No rice at home only trappings of a zamindar.

Proverb against showing off.
*ghare nei bhat, koncha teen hat*

No rice at home yet dhoti worn in style.
Proverb against ostentation.
Or

*pet jvale bhate, sonar angti hate*

Dying of hunger yet gold ring on fingers.

*chokher chamra nei*

Eye without skin

Proverb against shamelessness.

*Mukhe khub mithe, neem nishinda pete*

Sweet words and bitter thoughts.

Proverb against hiding true self.
*Gharer dhan phele parer dhan aglan*

Ignores own property to protect that of others.
Proverb against inconsiderate people.

*Bou bhanglo sara,*
*gelo pada pada*

Wife breaks a plate,
everybody comes to know about it.

Proverb against unjust criticism.

*apnar bela bhatkapad*
*parer bela lathi chapad*

Food and clothes for self

Proverb against selfishness.

*intti parley patkelti khete hay*

Throw a stone and get it back

Tit for tat.

*goru chhagal beche bhatar*

*gaday mager galar har*

Husband sells cows and goats
Gets necklace made for wife.

Proverb against henpecked husband.

*ma beche khay kalmi shak*

Mother sells creepers to buy food.

Proverb against neglect of mother.

As seen earlier, the wife in the family is always under attack and she vents her anger through proverbs like:

*Bhalo katha mone padlo anchate anchate*
*thakurjhike niye gelo nachate nachate*

Remembered while rinsing mouth (after meal)
Sister-in-law was taken away dancing (or waves)

The sister-in-law had been dragged away by a crocodile and such was the wife's hatred of her that she did not report it earlier.

*shashuri molo sakale*

*Kheye deye bela thake to, kandbo giye bikale*

Mother-in-law died in the morning

Shall weep in the evening if there is time after my meal.

Not that the wife is wholly harmless:

*shashuri maren gunto, bou beti pelo chhuto*

Mother-in-law gives a shove giving wife an excuse (to hit her back).

*satiny dile sonar gayna, more dile phanki*

Gold ornaments for co-wife, none for me.

*satin kete alta pori*

Shall cut the co-wife and dye the feet (figuratively with her blood).

To be ungrateful is a common folly. Proverbs that condemn this:

*adar kajer bela*
*darpar abahela*

Looked after when needed
Then ignored.

*kajer bela kaji*
*kaj phurule paji*

Treated as kaji (judge) when there is need
Need over, become a bad man.

Proverbs against habitual fault finders:
*Apan chhidra jane na, parer chhidra khonje*

Knows not his own holes (faults), searches for holes in others.

*apan dosh jhudi jhudi, parer doshe di tudi*

Have loads of faults, rejoice to find those in others.

*Apnar mukh apni dekh*

See your own face.

Against laziness:

*Kajer madhye dui*
*Khai ar shui*

Have only two functions
Eating and sleeping.

*Kajer bela bhage*
*Khabar bela age*

Runs away from work
First one to eat.

Proverb on unseemly conduct:

*teenkal giye ek kale theke*
*tobu abar korbe biye*

Spent three fourths of life
Still wants to marry.

Proverb against farce as justice:

*doi khelen ramakanta*
*bicharer belay gobardhan*

Ramakanta ate the curd
Gobardhan brought to justice.

Against dowry:

*koner bap bose bose chokher jale bhase*
*barer bap bose achhe pansho takar ashay*

Bride's father is flooded by tears
Bridegroom's father waits for his five hundred.

Against wayward Brahmin priests:

*Bamun dakshina dhare*
*Dhenkir namey puja kare*

Brahmin takes his fee
Offers prayers for the husking pedal.

And lastly the woman who once said,

*Kane dilam tulo*
*Pithe bandhlam kulo*
*Tora yata paris bal*
*Yata paris kilo*

Plugged ears with cotton
Tied winnow on back
Say, what you want
Beat as much as you want.

Ultimately loses patience to announce,

*Hoi ginni na chhuin handi*

Once I am mistress won't touch the pots (will do no work).

# 5

# Bengali Proverb and Its Structure

"Perhaps all over the world, the growth of human civilization was accompanied by the creation of the proverb in keeping with the contemporary manner of speech. It was born spontaneously in people's minds like the rhymes of old".[1]

Thus did Tagore speak of the proverb in his *chhele bhuano chhadal* and went on to add, "many smells, sounds, colours, hints of thought, scrapans of language, float around in our stream of consciousness and strike like lightning the minds of the thoughtful and sensitive to find expression in the form of humourous comments. With time these sayings took the shape of proverbs, in a sense they constitute a mass statement".[2]

The proverb is a complete sentence, structurally so divided as to have two halves, one visible and one hidden. Externally the sentence is just an expression of a feeling and what is concealed or intimate is the subject matter. Since the proverb is speech-dependent and a part of the oral tradition, its structure varies from one region to another. Even in Bengal where the main language is Bengali, the proverb has not been able to avoid regional touches, indeed it could not have done so. At times, over a passage of time the same proverb sees words getting changed. Thus the present day, *dushtu gorur cheye shunya goal bhalo*, (empty cowshed is better than a naughty cow) had spoken in the hoary past, in the Caryageeti and Sanskrit, of a naughty *brisha* or *balad*, meaning a bull. The message, however, has remained the same and *goru* can be stretched to mean both cow and bull.

And therein lies the main point. Time may change the form of the proverb but not its content. In the case of the proverb mentioned, its ancient form, *bar sun gohali ki mo dutthat balande*, perhaps would have remained unknown if Caryageeti had not been discovered.

There are few languages as flexible as Bengali, a quality which has given it great powers of assimilation. As Sushil Kumar De has shown, Sanskrit part proverbs like *stribuddhi pralayankori* (woman's wisdom is disastrous), shubhashya shighram (sooner the better) entered Bengali with as much ease as the Hindi, *pahele darshandhari Pichhe gunbichari* (first see then judge). There are also *Pichhe gunbichari* proverbs with mixed words like,

*Compani Ka mal dariyame dal*

Company's property, throw it in the sea (is nobody's property).

Here the word 'company' is English.

There is a school which does not accept idioms and phrases as proverbs. But this is not quite correct. Phrases like *mathay akash bhenge pada* (skyu falling on the head, a disaster) or *tele begune jwaley otha* (fired up as brinjals in hot oil) are phrases come to become proverbs. In some cases only part of a proverb has, with time, come to be in circulation as the full proverb though that is not the case. Thus, *bhobi phulbar nay* (a stubborn man cannot be made to respond to entreaties) is not the whole proverb which is, *tel dao, sindur dao, bhobi bhulbar nay* meaning the person will not budge even if worshipped like a deity with oil and vermillion. Similarly, *yar yekhane byatha, tar sekhane hat* (touches he the spot where he is hurt) is preceded by the line, *achhad kheye pode gelo jan panch sat* (slips and fall five or seven) in the full proverb. In common usage, however, it is only the operative part that is quoted.

Dr. Sushil Kumar De has noted that proverbs are always in common, everyday language or *chalti bhasha.* This is the "language of homes, markets and fields". Rabindranath has called this language *kathyabhasha* or the spoken language.

The effectiveness of a proverb depends on how it is expressed and it is this everyday language that has given such strength to the Bengali proverb, making it bright, humorous, witty and of course mocking. Thus, *yubakale ranga kore briddhakale sati*—chaste in old age after a lot of fun in youth—is both sharply mocking as also hilariously funny.

A feature of the Bengali proverb is the use of rhetoric, both in terms of sound and meaning. Atttration, for instance, makes the proverb sound sweet, as in:

*Kajer name kaji, akaj pelei raji*

Here the repeated use of the alphabet 'j' gives a pleasant ring to the proverb.

Then here is the double meaning:

*Kul to nay, kuler anti*

The word 'kul' has been used first to mean clan and then the jujube.

The proverb aims at disparaging lineage, saying it is nothing more precious than the seed of a jujube.

Then some comparisons, metaphors, allegory, simile etc. For instance, *jyestha bhrata sama pita* (elder brother is like the father) or *ek mayer ek put, khay day yena yamer doot* or only child of mother eats like yama's messenger. Then in *apnar charkay tel dao* or oil your own spinning wheel, we find exaggeration as the spinning wheel represents work in general and what the proverb is really saying is, mind your own business. The use of metaphor is seen in, *uthan samudra par hoa* in which the *uthan* or courtyard is seen as *samudra* or the sea which has to be crossed. There are also proverbs which are sarcastic, censure appearing in the garb of praise :

*thakuraner garbha chamatkar*
*biyechhen ek bandar abatar*

Lady has a fine womb
Given birth to a monkey incarnate.

Proverbs in rhyme form are not just nursery rhymes but to make the everyday prose sound sweeter. To quote

Rabindranath, "when word stands straight, it imparts only its meaning, but when it is given a shake with rhythm then something more than the plain meaning is got". This is what the rhythmic proverb does, it gives more than the meaning of the words as can be had in the lexicon. The rhythm here is that which can be had in folk songs, in the chant of *bratas,* outside the pale of literature. It is, again as the poet termed it, popular rhythm. It is uniform rhythm, the uniformity achieved by adjustments in pronunciation. Like:

1 1 1 1 1 1 1 1 1 1 1 1 1 1
*natun notun / khaier moa / kachar machar kore I = 14*

new parched rice sweets make a sound when eaten

At times of course the uniformity is broken:

1 1 1 1 1 1 1 1 1 2 1 1 1
*Purano hole khaier moa I = 14 noaia pade*

when old parched sweets bend down.

In the second line, the syllables in *purano* are three but become two when pronounced fast. Three syllables in again *noaia* become four because of the extended manner of pronunciation. The whole proverb is a couplet in the *payar* metrical system in which each line has fourteen syllables.

There are many examples of proverbs in the *payar* rhythm. Such as:

1 1 1 1 1 1
*Shunle kathar chhandd*

1 1 1 1 1 1 1 1 1 2 1 1 1
*Handi bhenge mach palalo jhol railo bandha*

Hearing the rhythm of words

Of breaks, fish escapes, cooking remains stopped. In *railo* the two syllables have become three because of the extended pronunciation.

Variations within uniformity are also to be found:

*Bo-u bhanglo sara, gelo pada pada*

*ginni bhanglo nada, o nay dada kichhu*

Wife breaks plate, news spereads all over

Lady of the house breaks, oh that is nothing.

Proverbs are mostly of six. Eight or twelve syllables:

1 1 1 1 1 1
*Kshirer handir machi*

The fly in the pot of *Khir*

1 1 1 1 1 1 1 1
*Kshirer bhitar hirar chhuci = 8*

diamond knife in *khir* (concluted in sweet terms).

Repetitions also enrich proverbs :

*uchit kathay devta tushta, uchit kathay manus tushta*

Just words please gods, just word please man.

Also opposites :

*ajnaner pap jnane yay, jnaner pap tirthe yay*

Sin of the unwise go with wisdom, sin of the wise go with pilgrimmage.

There are proverbs in couplet form, the meaning getting clear in the second line:

*tas, daba, pasha, tine sarbanasha*

Cards, chess, dice, three bring disaster.

yekhane geraster basa, sekhane atithir asha

where lives the householder, there guests have hope,

Sometimes the first line is of one word and it rhymes with the last word of the next line ;

chacha, apan pran bancha

uncle, Save your own life. (Self before all else at times of trouble).

*dhoba, parer kapar shoone*

fasherman beautifies others' clothes.

With time proverbs also undergo slight changes in language:

*nai mamer cheye, kana mama bhalo* has today become, *nei mamar....* The meaning is, blind uncle better than no uncle, or something is better than nothing.

The use of the negative and word repetitions also make proverbs interesting:

*ek put, put nay, ek kodi kodi nay,*

*ek chokh chokh nay*

One son is no son, one cowrie is no cowrie

one eye is no eye.

Words not very common also find place in proverbs:

*bheng marte sonar kanr*

bheng is *byang* or frog and *kanr*, spear.

Proverb means, golden spear to kill a frog.

Some proverbs are marked by absence of verbs :

*andher nadi, kripaner kodi*

Blind man's stick, miser's money.

*baman haye chande hat*

Dwarf seeking to reach for the moon.

*Shakher pran gader math*

Happy heart is like vast green space.

Proverbs with compound verb:

*garabe beti amar buk phuliye hante*

Daughter walks swelling in pride.

Infinite verb:

*hese hese katha kay, e hasi bhalo nay*

Talks Iaughing, this laugh not good.

Use of noun:

*hater lakshmi paye thela*

Kicking aside Lakshmi at hand ignoring opportunity.

*kapal gune gopal thakur*

Gopal, thanks to fate (Gopal is Krishna).

One of the characteristics of proverbs is rhyming lines and non-rhyming lines:

*ekkale anuragi*
*ar ekkale bairagi*

At one time a devotee
At another time a stoic.

Non-rhyming:

*yar mukhe bish*
*tarjiv chhenra*

Whose words are poisonous
Has a cleft tongue....

In some proverbs it is the same person who asks a question and then answers it. Like:

*bouer chalan keman*
*na, turki ghoda yeman*

How walks the wife?
Like a Turkish horse.

Then there are those like a statement:

*kana chheler nam padmalochan*

Blind boy called lotus-eyed.

Some proverbs carry words which are sound related. Like *tiptip* or flickering, *chadchad* or scratching.

Then there is the use of the onomatopoea like the words *nade chade*. Then there is the repeated use of the same word:

*eksathe elam panch bhai*
*sheshe dekhi thain thain*

Here the word repeated is, *thain.* The proverb means:

Five brothers came together
Then they fought.

In Bengali there is the *bahubrihi samas*, a word formed by joining two words and conveying a meaning which is not that of the words taken separately. Thus, proverbs like:

*kanakanir par janajani*

First whispered then common knowledge.

Then proverbs with the nominal verb:

*ye yare dhay, se tare pay*

Whom he chases, gets him.

here *dhay* is the nominal verb.

A living language, Bengali has many foreign words incorporated in it and this is seen in proverbs also:

*kajir goru khoda rakhal*

Judge's cow, shepherded by God

Here *Kaji* and *Khoda* are foreign words.

*mollar doud masjid paryanta*

Mullah's influence is upto the mosque.

Molla and masjid are foreign words.

Then there is the use of words having opposite meaning:

*ati pirit yekhane, ati bichhed sekhane*

Great love leads to great separation.

*agey sanchay parey byay*

First save then spend

Numbers in words feature in many proverbs to highlight the message sought to be conveyed. For instance, a professional godman would appear in a manner which would raise the fee for being in his presence:

*kapale lamba phonta, darshani choddo taka*

Long sacred mark on forehead, fourteen rupees the price of a visit.

*kaner baap bose bose chokher jale bhase*
*barer baap bose achhe panchsho takar ashe*

Tears flood the bride's father
Groom's father waiting for his five hundred rupees.

Western folk culture specialists have analysed the structure of the proverb in many ways. Alan Dundas has spoken of topic and comment as the basis of the proverb:

*nachte na janle uthon byanka*

don't know dancing, blame the courtyard.

Here the first part is the topic and the second the comment.

Noam Chomsky has pointed out discipline and unity which has brought uniformity in the subject and structure of proverbs the world over. Again Alan Dundas, taking a cue from G.B. Milner, has, from the point of view of meaning, divided proverbs into the oppositional and non-oppositional. Instances of the oppositional:

*geon yogi bhikh pay na*

Known yogi gets no alms (familiarity breeds contempt).

*khonda pa khale pade*

Lame leg falls in the ditch.

And the non-oppositional:

*ganye mane na, apni modol*

Calls himself boss but nobody obeys.

Paul D. Goodwin and Josep W. Wenzel have identified features that mark the thought process of the proverb maker:

Sign: *Shikari bidal gomfe chena yay*

Hunting cat known by its moustache. The moustache is the sign.

Number: *ek dhile dui pakhi mara.*

Killing two birds with one stone.

Cause and Effect: *pete khele pithe say*

Full stomach, back can take a beating.

Motivatin: *nijer nak kete parer yatra bhanga kara*

Harming self to spite another.

Parallel: *sap hoye kate, ojha hoye jhade*

Bites like the snake, curse like exorcist.

Analogy : *tumi thako dale dale, ami bedai patay patay*
You in the branches, I among the leaves (I can outsmart you).

Generalization : *ye yay lankay, se hay ravana*
He who goes to Lanka becomes Ravana (Power corrupts)

Classification : *chore chore mastuto bhai*
Thieves are as thick as cousins,

Pairs : *samayer ek phond, asamayer dash phond*
One stitch at right time is ten at the wrong time (stich in time saves nine).

The conclusions arrived at by Ashoke Kumar Dey regarding the structure of the proverb are also worth looking into:

(a) Proverb is the symbol of a mood.

(b) Proverbs are all of one sentence, sometimes simple sometimes compound.

(c) Proverbs are bright examples of folk language and manner of speech.

(d) The language is easy and the style of presentation is simple.

(e) Proverbs say little but convey much more.

Discipline of thought and structure is the essence of the proverb, it cannot be constructed haphazardly. Scientific reasoning is its basis.

## References

1. Tagore, Rabindranath, Loksahitya, 1378, p. 7.
2. Tagore, Rabindranath, Loksahitya, pp. 7-8.
3. Tagore, Rabindra Rachanabali, West Bengal Govt. Pub., Part X, p. 994.

# 6

# Proverbs and Folk Literature

It is easy to find similarities between all forms of folk literature, such as rhymes, riddles, proverbs, ballads, stories because these are all drown from everyday experience of life. But even then the proverb stands apart as it is the shortest expression of thought born out of that experience and in this regard it has no parallel. Let us examine the proverb in the context of folk literature as a whole.

## Riddle and Proverb

The riddle is a single question posed with the help of mataphor and allegory, while the proverb, as said earlier, is the shortest expression of lessons learnt from experience over a long period of time. Structurally they enjoy close similarity and some riddles have come to be accepted as proverbs, such as:

*kiba desher goon, eki gachhe pan, supari,*

*eki gachhe choon*

What a land, same tree grows betel leaves, betel nuts and lime.

This is a riddle, the answer being banyan tree.

As a proverb it mean somebody who is self sufficient.

Again some riddles have qualities of the proverb:

*Chhai bhinna shoy na, lathi bhinna othe na*

Sleeps but only on ash, gets up but only when kicked.

As a riddle, the answer is dog and as a proverb it means a useless person.

Both the riddle and the proverb can be seen in either prose or verse form.

Prose form:

Proverb : *ghare nei khad, dhenkishale parchala*
No straw in the room, threshing yard well covered.

Riddle : *han achhe, hun nai, much achhe magaj nai*
Has face, no word, has head but no brain.
The answer is, doll.

Verse form:

Proverb : *khartar nari, jharjhar jhari*
*chor, nafar, pad pad ghar*
*tak nati durat sar*

raueous woman, leaking pipe
thieves, servants
keep away from them.

riddle : *aganan pao tar*
*Raanga baran deha*
*Na bolibe keha*

Countless legs it has
Body is red
Goes where it wants
None to stop it.

Answer : Earthworm.

The proverb is concerned with active life, the riddle is for leisure moments. The proverb brings with it fruits of experience, the purpose of the riddle is to amuse.

Some examples:

Proverb : *fagune diye chaite diye mati aagun*
*baanshti kahe uthi uthi*

Fire in falgun, fresh earth in chaitra the bamboo begins to raise its head.

This is advice backed by experience.

Riddle : *dhala mian haate yay*
*nitya haate chimti khay*

White man goes to market

Is pinched everytime.

Answer: Bottle gourd or *laau.*

Here the purpose is to provide amusement.

The language of the proverb is sharp, satirical, of the riddle picturesque.

Proverb : *pare na kochu kate, aage dhay ende kutte*
Can't cut roots, goes to tackle a bull.

Riddle : *bon theke berulo tiye*
*sonar topar mathay diye*

Comes parrot from the forest
Gold crown on head.

Answer : Pineapple.

Both the proverb and riddle are marked by terseness, more so the

Proverb : *kane jal dileyi jal beroy*

Water in ear brings water out.

Riddle : *etatuku mithai, ghar bhore chhitai*

Little sweet that I spread throughout the room.

Answer : Light.

The proverb advises, riddle speaks of a material thing.

Proverb : *panch kaje dibe mon*
*Sab kaje jhan jhan*

Try to do too many things
Spoil everything.

Riddle : *ajagar naiko ami, enke benke choli*
*pathe pathe pani khai ugle abar pheli*

Not a python but zigzag I go
Swallow water on way and throw it out.

Answer : Train.

Unlike the riddle the proverb deals with harsh reality:

*betay rakhe nam*
*bitit dyakhay gram*

Son is the pride of the clan
Daughter of the village.

The message is, in the family the son counts for more than the daughter.

Riddle : *etir madhye oti diye*
Mag bhatare railo shue

Putting that in this
Wife and husband went to bed

Answer : Door bolt.

Women feature in both the proverb and the riddle but less so in the latter:

Proverb : bouti bhalo bate

tkna khaye batna bate

good indeed the wife is

grinds spices even after abuse.

Riddle : *boli bhalo manusher jhee*

*tomar byaparkhana ki*

*dite giye roye gele*

*arey chi, chi, chi*

My good girl

What's wrong with you

About to give, then stopped

Shame on you.

Answer : About to cover her head with sari end then stopped.

Another proverb on women:

> *nodir jemun joar bhanta*
> *maior yaubon paner bonta*
>
> like ebb and tide of river
> Woman's youth is stalk of betel leaf.

Youth is not permanent, it dries up and dies like the leaf-stalk.

Variety of subjects mark both proverbs and riddles,

Proverb : *bidhir neka jeevan joda*
*yemun sahis temun ghoda*

The Lord's writing is all over
As is the groom so is the horse.

This is an example of a philosophical observation. The riddle deals with more common subjects:

> *dui haat tuliya, madhye dilam bhariya*
> *kajti dilam sariya*
>
> Raised both hands and inserted it
> Finished the work.

Answer, Putting in the hairpin.

> *Lagel gelò*
> lege ailo
> *bajare gi*
> *pet bhorlo*
>
> went with me
> Returned with me
> In the market
> Filled his tummy.

Answer : Oilcan.

Proverb is always direct while a riddle can be either direct or indirect:

Proverb : *yadi bale paker katha, othe mattar byatha*
If asked to cook, develops headache.

Riddle (direct) : *kancha khao paka khao khaite mishti*
*ami yadi boli khao chote karo ansrishti*

Eat raw, eat ripe, tastes sweet
If I say eat it, create havoc,

Answer : Banana. In Bengal to ask somebody to eat a banana is to insult him.

Riddle (indirect) : *e parate budi mare*
*o paratey gandha chhore*

Old woman dies on this bank
Small reaches other bank.

Answer : Jackfruit.

The riddle often carries unnecessary words to confuse the listener but not so the proverb which is essentially disciplined. Thus the riddle:

*hajar takar morich khaia aro khaite chay*

Eats pepper of thousand rupees yet wants more

Answer : Grinding stone. This is the operative part but there is a preceding line about a tree in the palace which is redundant.

The proverb states only what experience has shown to be the truth. The riddle, on the other hand, contains both truth and exaggeration:

Proverb : *randhunir sange pirit thakle bhojanete sukh*
Friendship with the cook makes meals enjoyable.

Riddle : *dui mukhe katha kay thappad yadi khay*
Speaks with two mouths if slapped.

Answer : Drum.

The proverb is small in size with a wide message. In the case of the riddle both the size and message are limited:

Proverb : *ek hate tali baje na*

Can't clap with one palm.

Riddle : *handar bhitar mahish gonshay*

Buffao groans in a pot.

Answer : the *ghungur* or ankle-bell.

Proverb : *dhenki swarge geleo dhan bhane*

Husking pedal works even when in heaven.

Riddle : *gangparer budi nao dhan kute*

*kaankalite* pad dile kekkat kori uthe

Old woman husking paddy by riverside

Shove in the waist makes her groan.

Answer : Husking pedal.

Both have come down through ages yet-retain contemporaneity:

Proverb : *sargochali bou*

kame ni day mon

Gallivanting women has no time for work.

Riddle : *dui chal ek bati*
*bole dao tar nam ki*

Two roofs one stick
Say what is it?

Answer : Banana leaf.

The proverb is marked by its meaning of the riddle by descriptive quality:

Proverb : *bap mar ashubad*
*kha bacha ghee o bhat*

Blessings of parents on you
Eat child clarified butter (ghee) and rice.

Riddle : *gacher nam hira, katak hay pan supari,*
*katak hay jira*

Tree grows betel leaves and betel nuts
As also cummins.

Answer : kadam tree.

In both cases sound and meaning help identify some external signs:

Proverb : *ye pishe se yane*

Only he knows who suffers.

Riddle : *phool hay shata shata, phal hay baroda*
*pakli ekta*

Flowers in hundreds, fruits twelve
Only one when ripe.

Answer : Days, months, year.

Both the proverb and the riddle are essentially factual:

Proverb : *sambal rekhe kheo*
*bela thakte badi yeo*

When eating keep something in store
Go home while it is still light.

Riddle : *pancjane tule dile batrishjaner pare*
*sakalke ek jane tene nilo ghare*

Five lift it on thirty two
One pulls it all home.

Answer : Five fingers, thirty two teeth, one tongue.

Proverb and Rhyme:

Both are found in everyday colloquial language, enjoy the power of description and are marked by alliteration, rhyming. Unlike the rhyme, the proverb can be both in prose and verse. Also the range of subjects is much more in proverbs than in rhymes.

Some examples of this:

Family Relations

Mother : *chinda balo mudi balo bhater bada nai*
*masi balo pisi balo mayer bada bai*

Be it chira or muri mothing like rice
Be it mother's sister on
Father's nothing like mom.

Son's wife : *kaj nei bou kaj kore*
*dhane chale ek kore*

Wifepare us your efforts
You are mixing the rice with the paddy.

Mother and wife :

*Maer peter bhat nei,*
*bouer chandra har*

Mother starves,
wife wears fancy necklace.

Daughter : *meye nay ta sat beta,*
*meyer biyey korbo ghata*

Girl like seven sons,
will marry her off with pomp.

Social life :

Relation through marriage :

*emon kutum kothay pai*
*gada khan thuiye leja khan khay*

Where to get such a relation
Will eat the tail, leaving aside the fleshy part (of fish).

On love : *natun natun khoier moa machar machar kare*
*purano holey khoier moa pare netaia*

Fresh parched rice is crunchy

When old becomes limp.

Love loses flavour with age.

The rhymes on the other hand are far less varied. The most common is the lullaby and those associated with children's games.

Lullaby : *kendo na sonamani*
*kandle gala bhangbe*
*rat pohale banshi debo*
*yata sonar lagbe*

Cry not my dear
You will crack your voice
Give you toys in the morning
As many as you want.

There are rhymes which have to be chanted on occasions like the observance of women's rituals. There are no occasion-specific proverbs. These are about life in general.

In a proverb the statement is indirect but not so in rhymes:

Proverb : *padmamukhi jhi amar parer ghare yay*
*khendanaki bou ese batay pan khay*

My lotus-faced daughter goes to another's home

Comes snub nosed wife to eat betel leaves from the bowl.

Here the attitude towards son's wife is made clear in an indirect manner,

Rhyme : *rag koro na, ami tomar meye shashudi,*
*tumi yadi tarao tabe dandai kotha yeye*

Be not angry mom-in-law I am your daughter
If you throw me out where shall I find shelter?

Doubts and suspicion mark the proverb, faith the rhyme:

Proverb : *jomi kino kandar*
bou kino bandar

Buy land and weep
Buy monkey for wife.

Rhyme : *tai, tai, tai*
*masir bari yai*
*masir badi bhari maja*
*keel chad nai*

Clap, clap, clap
Going to aunt's house
Great fun there
No blow or slap

In some cases the message in the rhyme is similar to that in the proverb:

Proverb : *shashudi nai nanad nei kar ba kori dar*
*agey khai pantabhat she she lepi ghar*

No mom-in-law, no sister-in-law whom do I fear
Shall first eat rice then clean the room.

Rhyme : *Shashudi nai, nanad nai kare kormu dar*
*agey barmu bhija bhat, pare mujmu ghar*

The meaning is the same as in the proverb.

Another form of folk literature is the ballad which of course by its very nature is totally different form the proverb. The ballad is meant to be sung, rhythm is the main component of its composition which is not the case with a terse statement which the proverb often is. Also the ballad tells a tale of romance, which is not the purpose of the proverb, and hence cannot be as short as the latter. The language of the ballad is light which is not the case with the proverb.

# 7

# Proverbs in Bengali Literature Selected Examples and Analysis

The use of proverbs dates back to Sanskrit literature and these are found in the works of Kalidasa, Sudraka or Banvatta, particularly in conversation among women. In the second act of Kalidasa's Aviganyam Sakuntalam we come across a proverb the translated version of which into English would read, 'boil on top of filana' meaning added trouble and which is commonly used in today's colloquial Bengali (Goder upor bishfonra). Such proverbs makes us assume that the court poets in those days had not lost contact with the common people and drew from the experience of daily life. Through such usage was established a link between the commoner and upper echelons of society as it existed then and helped in the creation of a literary tradition that was not restricted to any particular section. In the case of the proverb the tradition was essentially popular and was carried forward like an endless stream to make its acceptance universal. This is what called Social Persistence.

Such persistence can be noticed in modern or pre-modern Bengal literature, with poets and artistes carrying forward the culture traditions of their individual clans. At times the manner of expression gets dispersed or radiated as a ray of light. In pre-modern on in modern Bengali literature, some unputdownable subjects have been used frequently. Belifs, rituals & rites, sermons and hymns, and linguistic expression of social aspects are eternal. Therefore, modern or pre-modern poets and artists are still now carrying their stream of culture in their works. Somewhere, these traditions are living, and somewhere these are scattered. The radiance of tradition is called the culture gene.

Literary use of proverbs began a thousand years ago when Bengali literature of today had its birth. They are found in Buddhist songs and couplets and are considered as the first literary proverbs of our literature. Some examples:

*hathere kankan ma lou darpan*

No need to consult a mirror to see if bangle is there.

*apna mangse harina bairi*

Its flesh makes deer its own enemy

*haadit bhat nanhi niti abeshi*

No rice in pot yet guests come everyday.

*duhil dadhu ki bente samaha*

Can milk drawn out re-enter the udder.

Many such proverbs are still in circulation with slight alterations. As are those to be found in Sri Krishna Kirtan Kavya.

*Makader hate jehnu jhuna narikel (dankhanda)*

Mokey with a coconut the ape can only throw it and hurt others.

*ye thane shunchi na jane tatha batia banae* (tambukhand)

Trying to put in a rope where a needle cannot enter.

*latat likhit khdan na jae*

What fate has ordained cannot be changed. (*dankhanda*).

*hath badhailen ki chander lag pai*

The moon remains out of reach (*bharkhanda*)

*dekhiyan sadhur dhan chor pudi more*

Seeing saint's wealth thief burns himself to death.

Of Jealousy most probably.

*pat patiyan kenhe nahi deha bhat* (*Vrindabankhanda*)

Having arranged the plate why aren't you serving the food?

Why are you disappointing me.

*yar skandhe base doshar matha (Kaliadaman khanda)*

Only those with two heads on shoulder can speak to Radha.

A task impossible for an ordinary man.

*ye dale karo mo  bhare*

*se dal bhangiyan pare (Radha viraha khanda)*

Branch on which I sit.

Breaks down.

Hapless person.

**Ramayan : Krittibas**

*pimpirar pakha uthe maribar tore*

Ants grow wings to die.

Proverb speaks of vaulting ambition.

**Mahabharat : Kashiram Das**

*agni, byadhi, wrin—e teener rekho na chin*

Fire, illness, loan—cure fully leaving no trace.

*parey nind, nahi dekho chhidra apnar*

Finding others' faults, blind to his own.

Akin to, pot calling kettle black.

*byaghra nahi janma lay mrigir udare*

Tiger not born in an eplileptic's womb.

*swami bina akaran narir jeevan*

Woman's life pointless without husband.

**Srikrishna Vijay : Maladhar Bosu**

*nirdhan purusher bhay nahik samsare*

Poor man has none to fear.

*karnadhar bine kabhu nouka nahi yay*

Boat cannot move without oarsman.

*Janani jathare duksha na yay khandan*

Sorrow of mother's womb cannot be removed.

**Mansa Mangal : Bejoy Gupta**

*bine sudddhite ghare gele loke na bale*

People condemn those who enter the house without

cleaning themselves.

**Padma Purana : Narayandeva**

*balaker muke yena jhuna narikel*

*kaker mukete yena dekhi paka bel*

Like a ripe coconut in a boy's mouth

Like a ripe bel fruit in a crow's mouth.

Impossible, both are too hard for either the boy or the crow.

**Manasa Mangal : Ketkadas khemananda**

*bipatter kale keha nahi mile sakha*

At times of crisis friends disappear

**Chandi Mangal : Mukunda Chakravarty**

*jamma lavile abashya achhe maran*

If born then death must come

*dughda diya ki karane posho kal sap*

Feeding milk to a poisonous snake.

*apni rakhile ray apnar man*

You alone can safeguard your prestige.

*daridre keha na sambhase*

Nobody the poor addresses (cares for)

*uchit kahite ami sabakar ari*

My just words have made me enemy of all.

Abhaya Mangal: Dwijaram Das: *purush kathin yati hirar kathari*

Men are hard like a diamond chopper.

**Shibayan : Ramakrishna Kavichandra**

*grihaster dharma nahe shmashan nivas*

Crematorium no home for a family man.

*poda ghaye pade yena labaner chhita.*

Adding salt to injury.

*stribuddhi pralayankari hena kahe bede*

Women's counsel is dangerous, it is said in the Vedas.

**Dharma Mangla : Rupram Chakravarty**

*asatya saman pap nahika samsare*

No sin greater than lies.

Gorkha Vijaya :

*shakti bina srishti kare kar emon shakti*

Who has the power to create without power?

**Satimoyna O Lorchandrani Kavya : Daulat Kazi**

*kripaner dhan yena murkher youban*

Miser's wealth is like the fool's youth.

*purush bhramara jati sambhram na ede*
*yei phule madhu pay tatha giya pade*

The male bee has no sense of prestige
Sits on whichever flower has honey

*kandari bihin nouka arote bhang hay*

Boat without oarsman collapses in current.

**Annada Mangal : Bharatchandra**

He is the best so far as literary

Proverbs are concerned:

*nagar purile devalaya ki eray*

When the city burns is the temple spared?

*kodite bagher dudh miley*

Money buys even tiger's milk.

*bador piriti balir bandh*
*kshaneke hate dodi kshanake chand*

Love of the powerful is a sand embankment
Now ties the hands now gives the moon.

**Padavali : Ramprosad Sen**

*matha nei matha byatha*

No head but headache

*kil kheye kil churi*

Tit for tat.

*khundite kenchua pachhe uthe kal sap*

Digging for snails, out comes a snake.

Unnecessary interference can lead to trouble

**Shunya Puran : Ramai Pandit**

*arao baghor bhoy jalat kumbhir*

Tiger on the bank crocodile in river.

**Padmavati : Alaol :**

*padoshi hoile shatru grihe such nai*

Neighbour turns foe, no peace at home.

*agey duksha sahile paschchate sukh pay*

sufferings lead to happiness

**Layli Majnu Kavya : Daulat Ujir Baharamkhan**

*yei taru pholiba ankure bhalo hoye*

Good seed gives good fruits.

*kaker mukhete yena sinduria aam*

ripe red mango in crows beak

Something that is wasted.

*mriter upar kharga uchit na hoy*

Strike not the dead

Speak no evil of the dead.

**Dasarathi Roy (1806-1857)**

*mukhe madhu antare bish*

Honey-tongued, poison inside

*ka akshar go mansa*

Alphabets untouchable as beef.

An unlettered person.

*eke manasa tay dhunor gandha*

First the snake goddess

then on top of it incense.

To add to trouble. The snake is further annoyed by the smell of incense.

**Gopal Uriya (approx. 1819-1859)**

*gachhe kanthal gonfe tel*

Twirling moustache seeing Jackfruit on tree.

Counting chickens before they are hatched.

Proverbs are to be found not just in ancient literature or the literature of the middle ages, later and modern day writings also abound in them. Examples:

**William Carey (1761-1834)**

*dudhe alta rang*

Lac-dye milk complexion.

Very fair.

**Mrityunjoy Vidyalankar (1762—1819)**

*gaddalika prabaha*

Floating with the tide.

**Tekchand Thakur (1814-1883)**

*er mundu or ghade*

His head on another's shoulder.

To confuse things.

*aranye rodan kara*

To cry in the forest.

To appeal in vain.

**Iswarchandra Vidyasagar (1820-1891)**

*uday sankat*

Caught in a cleft stick.

Kaliprasanna Singha (1840-1870) :

*Kanchite bongsholochan janmano*

Tabasheer born in bamboo twig.

Noble birth in a lowly family.

**Dwijendranath Tagore (1840-1926)**

*purano chal bhate bade*

Old rice become more when cooked.

Experience is valuable.

**Mir Mosarraf Hossain (1847—1912)**

*bidal tapasvi*

Praying cat.

Pretending to be honest and pious.

**Ramendrasundar Trivedi (1864-1919)**

*ahi nakul sambandha*

Relationship between snake and mongoose.

Bitter relationship.

**Panchkori Bandopadhyay (1866-1923)**

*dhake kathi pada*

To put stick to drum

To initiate a ritual, to create mass hysteria.

*hate handi bhanga*

To break the pot in the market

To let out a secret in public.

**Balendranath Tagore (1870-1899)**

*ati dwarpe hata lanka*

Excess pride brought down Lanka.

This warning against excess is found in many proverbs used by him.

*ati baad bedo na jhade pode yabe*

Grow too tall, storm will bring you down.

*ati bhakti chorer lakshan*

Excess respect sign of a thief.

*ati bado rupashi na pay bar*

Too beautiful a girl does not get a husband.

*anek sanyasite gajan nashta*

Too many sanyasis spoil the show.

To many cooks spoil the broth.

**Dakshinaranjan Mitra Mazumdar (1877-1957)**

*hente kanta upare kanta*

Thorns below and above.

Way of execution as found in fairy tales and with time a proverb.

*hobuchandra raja.*
*gobuchandra mantri*

Fathead king and stupid minister.
Fool seeking counsel from another fool.

**Ramnarayan Tarkaratna (1822-1886)**

*uttam madhya deoa*

To give good and proper (to give a sound beating).

**Madhusudan Dutta (1824-1873)**

*gatasya shocana nasti*

Pointless to think of what happened.

Don't cry over spilt milk.

*parer mathay kanthal bhanga*

To crack jackfruit on another's head

To profit at the expense of another.

*kather bedal hole ki hay, indur*
*tarate parlei holo*

Cat may be of wood as long as it can drive away the mice.

It is the end that matters.

**Dinabandhu Mitra (1830-1873)**

*thak bachhte gaon ujar*

Search for the crook leaves village empty.

*nijer charkay tel deoa*

Oiling one's own machine (here spinning wheel)

Mind your own business.

*jor yar muluk tar*

He who is powerful owns the land

Akin to, he who pays the piper calls the tune.

**Jyotirindranath Tagore (1849—1925)**

*baro mase tero parbon*

Thirteen festivals in twelve months.

Non-stop festivals. Reference to Bengali social life.

**Amritlal Bosu (1858-1929) :**

*dhan bhante shiber geet*

Singing to praise of Siva while husking paddy.
Raising irrelevant issues.

*chorke bale churi karte,*
*rihastha ke bale sajag thakte*

Asking thief to steal and householder to be careful.

Adopting double standards, running with the hare and hunting with the hound.

**Girish Chandra Ghosh**

*kan khada kara*

To lift the ear.

Anxious not to miss hearing something.

**Dwijendralal Roy (1863-1913)**

Who has two heads on his shoulder?

*kar ghare duto matha*

Who will dare commit such a misdeed?

**Kshirodeprasad Vidyabinode (1864-1927)**

*kathbiralir sagar bandha*

Squirrels bridging the sea.

Even ordinary people can help create something big.

**Iswarchandra Gupta (1812-1859)**

goder upar *bishphonra*

Poisonous boil on elephantitis. Adding to injury.

*phere hate, bate, mathey,*

Moves around in the market,

fields, everywhere.

*gharer dhenki kumir hoye ghatay kato aghatan*

Husking pedal becomes crocodile, causes disorder. Even harmless things can cause problems.

*Michhimichhi khete gelo bhuter begar*

Pointlessly worked free for the ghost.

Meaningless labour.

**Madhusudan Dutta** (In writings apart from plays and farce):

*ye rakshak se bhakshak*

Guard who is also the thief.

*trina gyan kara*

To treat as grass.

To be contemptuous.

*manihara phoni*

Snake without its jewel.

To be wild in sorrow.

**Biharilal Chakravarty (1835-1898)**

*jhal jhada*

To spend anger on somebody

**Dwijendranath Tagore (1840-1926)**

*hal chede deoa*

To let go of the rudder.

To give up all hope.

**Rabindranath Tagore (1861-1941)**

*dine dakati*

Daylight robbery.

A brazen act.

*pitta jvale yaoa*

To burn with indigestion.

To have ill humour aroused.

*komor bandha*

Tightening the belt

To jump into action with determination.

*sobure meoa phale*

Patience pays.

*mandhatar amol*

Days of Mandhata

Very ancient times.

*Madhuren samapayet*

Ending as sweet as honey.

*Pete khele pithe soy*
Full tummy tolerates beating.
Loss bearable if compensated in another way.

*ramrajatya*
Rama's kingdom
Happy, prosperous times.

*benabone mukta chhadrano*
Throwing pearls in the jungle
Throwing pearls before the swine.

*pete kshide mukhe laj*
Hungry yet shy
To shie away from expressing desire.

*turki nachon nacha*
Dancing like a Turk (Arabian horse)
To gesticulate in extreme agitation.

*kake niye gelo kan, kaker pichhane dhabman*
Chasing a crow hearing it has flown away with an ear.
To believe without reasoning.

**Kazi Nazrul Islam (1899-1976)**

*chorer upar rag bhunye bhat khaoa*
Angry with the thief, eating off the floor.
To inflict suffering on self, being angry with somebody.

*rakta heem hoa*
*Blood curdling.*

**Jivanananda Das (1899-1954)**

*dharmer kal batase nade*
Religion prevails.

**Annada Shankar Roy (1904-2002)**

*karur poush mas karur sarvanash*
Lucky month for some, for others disastrous.
One man's food is another's poison.

**Jasimuddin (1904-1976)**

*shankher karat*
Conch-shell saw
Cuts both ways, double edged sword.

*sat ghater jal ek kara*

Bringing together seven rivers.

Display of great power.

*ghughu dekechha phand dekho ni*

Seen the bird, not the trap

To forget there is somebody always more powerful.

**Bishnu Dey (1908-1979)**

*chacha apan pran bancha*

Uncle, save yourself.

Selfish attitude.

**Bankim Chandra Chattopadhyay (1838-1894)**

*ekti asadhe galpo*

A monsoon tale.

A fantasy.

*rajay rajay yuddha hay ulukharer pran yay*

Kings fight

Dies the grass.

It is the ordinary folk who suffers when the powerful fight happens.

*machh morechhe bidal, kande*

Fish dies, cat weeps

Shedding crocodile tears.

*bridhasya toruni visham*

Young woman in dangerous for the old.

*yar karma tare saje*

Only he should do what he is used to.

*bhat chhadaile kaker abhab ki*

Scatter the rice and there won't be any dearth of crows. If there is money there won't be any shortage of followers.

*Andhakare dhil mara*

Throwing stone in the dark.

Taking chances, not sure of success.

**Rajshekhar Bose (Parasuram-1860-1960)**

*kukurke lai dile mathay othe*

Fondle the dog he will jump on your head.

Lowly person should not be too encouraged.

**Sarat Chandra Chattopadhyay (1876-1938) :**

*kamini kanchan*

Women and gold.

Principal requirements of a sensuous person.

*Int marle patkelti khete hay*

Throw a stone and it will come back.

Retribution is inevitable.

*Ardale rajar ma keo dain baley*

Even king's mother is called witch behind her back

Nobody can avoid criticism even if not openly.

*katleo rakta nei kutleo mansa nei*

No blood or flesh even if chopped up.

A person wholly without resources.

**Anurupa Devi (1882-1958)**

*abujhke bujahabo kata, bodh nahi mone*

How to explain to one who refuses to understand.

**Tarashankar Bandopadhyay (1891-1971)**

*adhikontu na doshay*

No harm in added precaution.

*anabhyaser phonta kapale chadchad kare*

The unusual hurts.

*machher mayer putrashok*

Fish mother grieving for her son.

Another example of shedding crocodile tears as the fish has no relationship with the spawn.

*kare parile bagha phoring khay*

When in trouble the tiger eats even grasshoppers.

**Giribala Devi (1891-1983)**

*dhenki ke bujhaba kata, nitya dhan bhane*

How to explain to the husking pedal,

Husks paddy everyday.

Doing diligently what is expected of him.

**Bibhutibhusan Bandopadhyay (1894-1950)**

*akash theke pada*

Fall from the sky

To be taken by surprise.

**Dhurjati Prasad Mukhopadhyay (1894-1961)**

*amta amta kara*

To fumble.

**Bibhutibhusan Mukhopadhyay (1896-1987)**

*asaler cheye sud mishti*

Interest is sweeter than principal.

What is derived from it better than the main thing.

**Balai Chand Mukhopadhyay (Banaphool 1899-1979)**

*upar chalak*

Outwardly smart.

**Saradindu Bandopadhyay (1899-1970)**

*chhagal tarano brishti*

Rain to drive away goats.

Short lasting rain.

**Shibram Chakravarti (1902-1980)**

*ghodar dim*

Horse egg

Something absurd.

*Bina meghe bajrapat*

Lightning without clouds.

Bolt from the blue.

**Achintya Kumar Sengupta (1903-1976)**

*kan tanle matha ase*

Pull the ear, the head comes.

Capture one of two related things or persons and the other will follow.

**Abul Fazal (1906-1983)**

*du mukho sap*

Double mouthed snake.

One who speaks both for the complainant and the accused, one not to be trusted.

**Manik Bandopadhyay (1908-1956)**

*kala bou*

Banana wife.

A shy women who covers her head with the sari end reaching as low the banana leaves.

*machher tele machh bhaja*

Fring fish in its own oil.

Getting things done cheaply.

**Syed Mujtaba Ali (1904-1974)**

*rath dekha kala becha*

Seeing the chariot and selling bananas.

Getting more than one thing done on any occasion, using pilgrimage to good practical use.

**Buddhadev Bose (1908-1974)**

*dhak petano*

To beat the drum.

To make public with great fanfare, to eulogise somebody.

**Ashapurna Devi (1909-1995)**

*kath khad podano*

Burning wood and straw

To spend a lot of labour.

*aluthalu*

Disheveled.

**Advaita Mallabarman (1914-1951)**

*athai jale*

In deep water

In deep trouble.

*kurukshetra ghatano*

Creating Kurukshetra

Causing pandemonium.

**Syed Mustafa Siraj (1930-)**

*jata, lota, kambal*

*ye hay sadhuka sambal*

Matted hair, pot, blanket

These are a sadhu's possession.

*dumurer phool*

Fig flower

Something that can't be seen, person in hard to be found.

**Shanker (1933)**

*haate handi bhanga*

To break pitcher in the market

To make public.

**Bijon Bhattacharya (1917-1978)**

*neda ekbar beltalay yay*

Bald headed goes under the *bel* tree only once.

Man learns from experience, the hard *bel* fruit falling on his head teaches him his lesson.

**Salil Chowdhury (1922-1995)**

*bhitey ghughu chadano*

Getting wily men to move around the house.

To bring about somebody's disaster.

**Gourkishore Ghosh (1923-2000)**

*gharer kheye boner mosh tarano*

Eating at home and chasing wild buffaloes. To get busy unnecessarily without any possibility of return.

**Nirendranath Chakravarty (1928)**

*yata garje tata barshe na*

Does not rain as it thunders.

Empty bragging.

**Sukanta Bhattacharya (1926-1947)**

*bhuin phonr*

*Sprouting*

Suddenly coming up with no background, self professed leader.

**Shamsur Rahman (1929)**

*saper panch pa dekha*

Seeing five legs of the snake. To ask for the impossible.

**Moti Nandi (1931)**

*maday kakhano bhons bhons kore ghumay*

Does the dead body snore? To have absurd thoughts.

**Sankha Ghosh (1932)**

*khol nolche palte*

Changing cover and pipe. To completely overhaul.

*Jantay pishe mara*

To crush in the grinding stone. To torture (figuratively).

**Shakti Chattopadhyay (1930-1995)**

*marar upar khandar gha*

To strike a dead body

To attack the already defeated.

*pithe kulo bandha*

Tying winnow on the back

To suffer all attacks.

**Taraknath Gangopadhyay (1843-1891)**

*had ek jaygay mas ek jaygay*

Bones at one place, flesh at another.

To beat mercilessly

**Ramesh Chandra Dutta (1848-1909)**

*svasharire swargalabh*

Alive yet in heaven.

To enjoy unexpected fortune.

**Sirshendu Mukhopadhyay (1935)**

*akash patal bhaba*

Thinking of the sky and nether world.

In a reverie.

**Afsar Ahmed (1959)**

*chulochuli*

Pulling hairs, fighting.

Folk culturists these days prefer to call oral tradition, oral heritage. Whatever the term, the fact remains that this tradition or heritage is like oxygen in our lives, we are kept alive and fresh by it. To Francis Potter this is Living Fossil, it is over centuries old and yet living and found in writings of those in the pay of the East India Company down to the present day writers. Over the years some proverbs have had minor changes, such as *din dupure dakatti* being *dupure dakati* in Tagore's *Sonar Tori,* but the meaning has remained the same, daylight robbery or a brazen act.

# 8

# A Comparative Study of Proverbs : Bengali, Regional and International

India has a mixed society, the population including Indo-Aryan linguistic groups on the one hand and Dravids, Negrito, Mongoloid on the other. Each ethnic group has its own peculiar culture but despite apparent contradictions they all enjoy a common heritage, drawing from the puranas and the epices. Also, as the French anthropologist, France Boas has pointed out, irrespective of their race people from the same economic background enjoy a common response. Similarities can be noticed among different people and it is these which bind them together, and the similarity in folk culture, as seen from a study of such of its elements as proverbs and riddles, has attracted the attention of scholars.. That there has always been a link between the present Indo-European people and the Indo-Aryans of yore is clear from the similarities of various cultural ingredients.

This sameness in folk culture, both within the country and across the borders, can only fill us with wonder. The universality of culture brings us the picture of similarities as well as diversities. It is this universality that unites among diversity and this unifying force finds expression through proverbs of different languages. For instance:

Hindi : *ma mare, ma hi to pukare*

Bengali : *maye marey, ma bolei kande*

Mother beats the child and while crying out it takes the same mother's name. Proverbs in both languages draw attention to the role that the mother plays in the child's life. Thus, the Bengali proverb:

*pithe balo mithe balo, bhater bada nai*
*pishi balo, mashi balo, mayer bada nai*

Pie or sweet, nothing like rice

Aunts, paternal or maternal, none is comparable with. Similar is the place of the brother. The Hindi proverb says,

*bhaisa mit nahi, bhaisa dushman nahi*

No friend like brother, no enemy like brother.

The Bengali version echoes that thought,

*bhaier tulay mitra nei, bhaier tulya shatru nei*

As we have already seen from the Bengali proverbs, daughters were considered a burden to their parents. That this was not so just in Bengal, becomes clear from the proverb from Orissa:

*jhio maran, pita tiun, na mile roon*

Daughter's death brings sadness and then happiness.

The son-in-law is feted but only as long as the daughter is alive. Proverbs on the subject in different Indian languages:

*meye banchle jamaier adar* (Bengali)
*baha saile bedir muhapuru* (Oriya)
*Ladki banchegi to damad ayega* (Hindi)
*akkal irukki baraitan machchan urbu* (Tamil)
*magalu iddare marmaya inige sanmana* (Kannada)

To the married daughter, her mother-in-law is evil incarnate, not only in Bengal but throughout the country as can be seen from the proverbs: The Bengali proverb has the daughter-in-law saying that she will weep for her dead mother-in-law only after doing her chores and taking her meals and that too if there is time left for that. The Hindi proverb says, *sas mora marey, sasur mora jeo* or Let the mother-in-law die but the father-in-law must live. As for the torturing sister-in-law, both languages have proverbs warning her to keep in mind that she also has a similar person at her in-laws place :

*nander o nanad achhe* (Bengali)
*nando ki bhi nanad hoti hoi* (Hindi)

Similar are the proverbs in the two languages involving both the mother-in-law and the sister-in-law :

*shashuri nei nanad kar ba kori dar* (Bengali)
*sas na andi, aphi anandi* (Hindi)

Women also hated their co-wives but in Bengal, while hoping they would meet a sad end, they had never nursed any grudge against the husband. But not so in Orissa as is clear from the proverb :

*ghaita pachhe moru, soutni pachhe rand hou*

Let the husband die and the co-wife hecome widow.

And a Hindi proverb says, the mother-in-law earns a bad name if co-wives not get along :

*soutin me khaṭpat, sas badnam*

In an agrarian society the cow had a major role to play in the family. Proverbs in different languages say that the kick of the milch cow must be accepted :

*ye goru dudh dey tar lathi o bhalo* (Bengali)
*dudharu gai ki lath bhi bhali* (Hindi)
*ye gai dudh dey hei gaie latailesh bhala* (Chakma)

Given below are examples of same proverbs in Bengali and other languages:

### Sanskrit

In Sanskrit the proverb is known as *Sadukti, payobad, lokoba* and *abhanak.*

Bengali : *ati bhakti chorer lakshman*
Excess show of piety is the sign of a thief.

Sanskrit : *shathe shathyang samacharet*
Bengali : *dushter sange durbyabahar proyajan*
Pay back in his own coin.

Sanskrit : *muninancha matibhramah*
Bengali : *muni hrishidero bhul hay*
Even sages can make mistakes.

Sanskrit : *ati sarbatra barjayet*
Bengali : *ati dawrpe hat ιanka*
Too much of anything is bad.

Sanskrit : stri buddhih pralayakari
Bengali : *stri buddhi pralayankar*
Women's counsel brings disaster.

Sanskrit : *kubakyantan cha sourhidam*
Bengali : kubakya prayog korle bondhutta nasta hay
Evil tongue breaks friendship.

Sanskrit : *kashte phale*
Bengali : *kashta korle keshta mele*
Labour brings fruits.

Sanskrit : *banijye basati lakshmi*
Bengali : banijyai lakshmi
Commerce brings wealth (Lakshmi is the goddess of wealth).

Sanskrit : *ayam aro gandosyopori sphotoh*
Bengali : *goder upar bishphonra*
Boil on top of elephentitis (added trouble).

Sanskrit : *vish kumbham poyomukham*
Bengali : *mukhe madhu antare bish*
Sweet tongue, poison inside.

Sanskrit : *bahvarambhe loghukriya*
Bengali : Same
Much ado about nothing.

**Pali**

In Pali the proverb is *pobado* just as it is *probad* in Bengali. Many Pali proverbs are to be found in the Buddhist *jatakas.*

Pali : *ati khatang hi papakang* (Jarudpan Jataka 256)
Bengali : *beshi kichhui bhalo nay*
Excess is harmful.

Pali : *apatechittang na sambhajeshsha* (Putbhatta Jataka 223, Godha Jataka 333)
Bengali : *ye dilo antare byatha tar sange kiser katha*
What communication with him who has hurt my mind.

Pali : *appedke ba machchhanang* (Mugpakhak Jataka 538)
Bengali : *alpa jale punti machh pharphar kare*
Little fish thrive in shallow water.

Pali : *asadhusannibaso namo papo anath karo* (Dadhibahan Jataka 186)

Bengali : *asat samge sarbonash*

Bad company brings disaster.

Pali : *udarashma ahang duto* (Duta Jataka 265)

Bengali : *lobhe pap, pape mrityu*

Greed is a sin, sin brings death.

Pali : *natthi loko raho nam papkommong pokubbato*

Bengali : *pap bapkeo chhade na*

Sin spares not the father.

Pali : *ysdisang bapate beejong adisang harate phalang*

Bengali : *yeman karma teman phal*

Reap as you sow.

Pali : *taddnya ca paning paribajjayshma* (Vidura Pandit Jataka 545)

Bengali : *yar pade tar khay, tari bhitey ghughu chaday*

Harms the benefactor, cuts the hand that gives.

### Urdu

In Urdu the proverb is called *mohaora* or *jambul mishla.*

Urdu : *ap ruchi khana par ruchi parna*

Bengali : *nijer ruchite khao, parer ruchite saj karo*

Eat according to your taste, dress according to others'.

Urdu : *chirag tale andhera*

Bengali : *pradiper talay andhakar*

Darkness below the lamp.

Urdu : *gharka bedi lanka chai*

Bengali : *gharer shatru bivishan*

Enemy is within.

Urdu : *nach na jane angan tera*

Bengali : *nachte na janle uthan byanka*

Knows not dancing, blames the floor (poor workman blames his tools).

Urdu : *dine tara ginna*

Bengali : *dine tara gona*

Counting stars at day, day dreaming.

Urdu : *ap bhala jag bhala*

Bengali : *nije bhalo, jagat bhalo*

I am good, so is the world.

Urdu : *jyasa karoge oisa payoge*

Bengali : *yeman karbe teman pabe*

Will get as you do (reap as you sow).

Urdu : *jo jita ohi sikandar*

Bengali : *ye joyi se shaktishali*

Nothing succeeds like success.

Urdu : *amke am guthlio ki dam*

Bengali : *rath dekha kala becha*

Seeing holy chariot and also doing business (killing two birds with one stone).

**Hindi**

In Hindi the proverb is known severally as *kahabat, lokokti, muhabara, upkhan* and sayings as *kahabaten.*

Hindi : *dudh put kismet se*

Bengali : *dudh, sishu, adrishta nirvar*

Milk, child (quality and nature of) ordained by fate.

Hindi : mukh me madhu bagal me chhori

Bengali : mukhe madhu bhitare chhuri

Honey in mouth knife under arm.

Hindi : *ek hath se tali nahi bajti*

Bengali : *ek hathe tali baje na*

Can't clap with one plam

It takes two to quarrel.

Hindi : *paradhin swapnenu sukh nahin*

Bengali : *nirbharshcel sukh jane na*

Dependent knows not happiness.

**Oriya**

The proverb is rudhi proyog in Oriya:

Oriya : *pani pyiba chhani paisa neba gani*

Bengali : *ya korbe bhebe chinnte korbe*

Look before you leap.

Oriya : *dheer pani pathar kati*

Bengali : *yara dheer sthir tarai pratiyogitay joyi hay*

Slow and steady wins the race.

Oriya : *sundar triptir abasad nahi yete dekhu thile noa disu khai*

Bengali : *sundar bastu chira amander hay*

A thing of beauty is a joy forever.

Oriya : *dur pahad sundar*

Bengali : *yeta dekhte pachhi na seta sabcheye sabuj sundar*

Distant pastures are greener.

Oriya : *ga kania singhani naki*

Bengali : *gharer jiniser mulya nai*

Familiarity breeds contempt.

Oriya : *dwip tale andhar*

Bengali : *alor talay andhakar*

Darkness under the lamp.

Oriya : *ye desh yai se phal khai*

Bengali : *yasmin deshe yadachar*

In Rome do as Romans do.

Oriya : *chaluni kahe chhchanchi ki, toh pachhare gotie kana*

Bengali : *chaluni bale chhunch ke, tor pichhane kena phuto*

Pot calling the kettle black.

Oriya : *gyete hate tali baje nahi*

Bengali : *ek hathe tali baje na*

It takes two to tango.

Oriya : *bish kambhob payomukham*

Bengali : *mukhe madhu antare bish*

Honey-mouthed poison inside.

Oriya : *ga pori mal dhoba tu tharu*

Bengali : *porichhanata dhopai jane*

Washerman knows cleanliness.

Oriya : *deshke phank noike bank*

Bengali : *sab desh saman nay*

All countries not same

## Bhojpuri

In Bhojpuri also the proverb is known as *lokokti* or *kahabat.*

Bhojpuri : *abre ki bhayne bial sagro gaon matiye le dhailo*

Bengali : *shoshan kare asahay kore deoa*

Fleecing dry

Bhojpuri : *aile geile gar halukaile, paile kaul haluk*

Bengali : *otiparishram kore byartha hoa*

Excess labour leading to failure.

Bhojpuri : *apan deke burbak banke*

Bengali : *toma sab diye boka boncchhi*

Given all as a fool.

Bhojpuri : *madhur anche roti mitha*

Bengali : *alpa anche ruti mishti*

Low fire makes bread sweet.

Bhojpuri : *tin dinke chokra mujhe shikhaot bat*

Bengali : *se diner chhokra kaiha shekhay*

Born the other day teaching me how to talk (teaching grandmother how to suck egg).

Bhojpuri : *unish bish to bhaile chahe*

Bengali : *prakritite duto jinish ek nay*

No two things are the same.

Bhojpuri : *samachuk phir ka pachtani*

Bengali : *ye sujog hariye gechhe tar janya duksha kiser*

Cry not for lost opportunity (don't cry over spilt milk).

Bhojpuri : *chor ka angari mitha*

Bengali : *chorer kachhe koylao mitha*

To a thief even coal is sweet.

## Assamese

The *yojana fakra* of Assam are skin to proverbs and sayings of Bengal. Most prevalent are the agriculture related *dak* sayings and the proverbs reflect satire, humour and morals.

Assamese : *gyat nai chal bakli / madya khai teen tekeli*

Bengali : *sharir pushta nay kintu teen bela madya chai*

Weak flesh yet drinks thrice a day

Assamese : *melat thaki nakay ucit*

*pape pay kincit kincit*

Bengali : *ye sakaler samne uchit katha baley na, se papi*
Sinner is he who is afraid to speak the truth.

Assamese : *buk phate*
*mukh nuphute*

Bengali : *buk phate*
*mukh phute na*
Heart breaks but mouth remains shut.

Assamese : *satkanda ramayan pori sita kar bap*
The Bengali proverb is almost exactly the same and it means, asking silly questions is a sign of ignorance.

Assamese : *daney durgati khanday*

Bengali : *dan kore dukshma nash hay*
Charity removes sorrow.

Assamese : *apuni aponar shatru*

Bengali : *manush nijer doshe nijer shatru*

Man's faults make him his enemy.

**Tamil**

The proverb is *bhasanam* in Tamil.

Tamil : *panam endralu, pinmum ray tirukkum*

Bengali : *takar katha shunle marao han kare*
Mention money, even the dead opens his mouth.

Tamil : *ahal irundal nihal ururu kittabandal muttappa hai*

Bengali : *dure thakle galagali, kachhe thakle chulochuli*
Friends when apart, foes when close.

Tamil : *pambuk-pa-pal bartalum*
*adur rushandan kakkum*

Bengali : *sapke dudh khaoale se ugre bishyi dhale*
Though you feed milk to the snake it will still inject poison.

Tamil : *petta tay muderi*
*puchand taram sridevi*

Bengali : *garvadharini alakshmi*
*notun bou ma lakshmi*
Mother is illuck, new wife has good luck

Tamil : *ahattin-de, deyarme tunai*
Bengali : *agatir gati bhagvan*
God is the last resort.

Tamil : *ahambaram perumbaram*
Bengali : *ahankar pataner karan*
Vanity causes downfall.

Tamil : *aniellam adoyin pin*
Bengali : *kapod agey alankar parey*
Clothes first ornaments later.

Tamil : *illarme lellaram*
Bengali : *sansar sera dharma*
Maintaining family most pious act.

Tamil : *udattile urbu, nenjile pahai*
Bengali : *mukhe madhu hride bish*
Honey toungued, poisonous heart.

**Telugu**

Proverb is *samita* in Telugu.

Telugu : *gate talli edde tantri*
Bengali : *yar ghare dhan achhe tar khub demak*
He who has paddy (wealth) is proud.

Telugu : *nagli unna uru akni cherdu*
Bengali : *krishi jeevaner upay*
Farming sustains life.

Telugu : *ban lunte pantelu*
*le kunte mantalu*
Bengali : *yeman brishti teman phasal*
As is the rain so is the yield.

**Kannada**

Proverb is known as *gardegolu in Kannada.*

Kannada : *ati ase gati keddu*
Bengali : *asha bhanga hoa*
Losing hope.

Kannada : *akka sattare amabse nirdalu*
*annasattare hunname nilladu*
*hannuma badua tanaka amabase nilladu*
*amabase badua tanaka hunname nilladu*

Bengali : *amabasya-purnima karur janya apeksha kore na*
Full moon and darkness wait for none/ Time and tide waits for none.

Kannada : *arasana kanta ha gayitu, bittimachida ha gaiyi*

Bengali : *ek dhile dui pakhi mara*
Killing two birds with one stone.

Kannada : *edabhida kalu edaudu hecchu*

Bengali : *durbhagya ekla ase na*
Misfortune does not come singly.

Kannada : *kunialike tilia duddare angara ore*

Bengali : *nachte na janle uthan byanka*
Does not know dancing, blames the floor/ poor workman blames his tools.

Kannada : *kumbaar arnige orusa danye ge nimisa*

Bengali : *matir patra goda yeman kathin bhanga teman sahaj*
Hard to make a clay pot, easy to break it.

Kannada : *shittu tanage kedu samadhan parrige keru*

Bengali : *krodh param shatru*
Anger is the biggest enemy.

Kannada : *summa niddare odam batta*

Bengali : *chup kore thaka sabar janya bhalo*
Silence is golden.

Kannada : *hale niru oledu mashle ketta du*

Bengali : *pukurer jal bhalo kumir bhalo na*
Lake water is good, not the crocodile.

Kannada : *mudi gintha nadeya mellu*

Bengali : *shabder cheye kaj katha bole beshi*
Work speaks more than words.

Kannada : *hole yubhudhela honnala*

Bengali : *chakchak korlei sona hay na*
All that glitters is not gold.

Kannada : *jeevana alpakalika*
*kalleyi dhiragakalluka*

Bengali : *jeevan swalpasthyayi, jnan ananta*
Life is short, wisdom for ever.

Kannada : *sondar abheyi shakti, mugalange adhara kathi*

Bengali : *soundarya shakti, hasi tar astra*
Beauty is power, smile its weapon.

Kannada : *anumanbheyi jnanoa mula*

Bengali : *sandeha jnaner utsa*
Doubt is the root of knowledge.

Kannada : *hakki jannu adara ovini edoa manuksha nannu avana mathininda guru thi sutha thabeyi*

Bengali : *pakhi pojha yay gane, manush chena yay kathane*
Bird known by its song, man by his words.

Kannada : *uttama saohaneyi enadhendu nashabhagubhudillu*

Bengali : *bhalo kaj kakhano haray na*
Good deed is never lost.

Kannada : *kallikayeyi berru kahiyagidharu bidhuva hallu sihi*

Bengali : *jnaner utsa korun, phal modhur*
Source of knowledge is sad, fruit sweet.

Kannada : *anubhav bhillada kalikayeyi jintha kaliyadaye padeva anubhav mellu*

Bengali : *jnan bina abhigyata, abhigyata bina jnaner cheye bhalo*
Experience without knowledge is better than knowledge without experience.

Kannada : *snehitha nillada jeevan sayu bhaga pakkadaiaru ella bhamthay*

Bengali : *bandhubiheen jeevan yena sakshibiheen mrityu*

Life without friends is death without witness.

## Malayalam

Proverb is *palajole.*

Bengali : *guru chakshudata*

Preceptor gives eyesight (shows the way).

Malayalam : *bhallabhanu pullumayudham*

Bengali : *bichakshaner hater ghas kharger matan*

Grass in the hands of the sioe is like sword.

Malayalam : *akaleulla bandhuvinekkal stattulla sattu nallu*

Bengali : *kachher shatru durer bandhur ceye bhalo*

Enemy near at hand better than distant friend.

Malayalam : *vidyail ninnum vinayam*

Bengali : *vidya benoy dan kore*

Learning imparts humility.

Malaylam : *adhik mayle amrutam visham*

Bengali : *adhik sannyasite gajan nashta*

Too many cooks spoil the broth.

Malayalam : *adi assa gati kedu*

Bengali : *sab kichhu asha korle sab kichhu harano*

Hope for more lose everything.

Malayalam : *choteyala chilum chodai bhare*

Bengali : *purano abhyes kakhano mare na*

Habits die hard.

Malayalam : *akore ninal ekore pacha, ekore ninal akore pacha*

Bengali : *ya dekhini tar cheye ya peyechhi tai sundar*

What I have is better than what I haven't seen/bird in hand is better than two in the bush.

Malayalam : *aguvare iranal orumbare irikyanam*

Bengali : *parishram karo, apeksha korte shekho*

Toil and learn to be patient.

Malayalam : *minuddelam ponnalla*

Bengali : *chakchak korlei sona hay na*

All that glitters is not gold.

Malayalam : *mansundegil margam unda*

Bengali : *icchha thakle upay hay*

If there is a will there is a way.

Malayalam : *akakkannu turappikkan asan balyattiletta nam*

## Marathi

Proverb is *mahan* or *ana* in Marathi.

Marathi : *kitihi keltari parsala pane tinac*

Bengali : *yatai karo yerakam se rakam thakbe*

Try as much you will nature will remain same.

Marathi : *andher ayat kana raja*

Bengali : *andher cheye ek chokh kana bhalo*

One-eyed better than blind

Half a loaf better than no bread.

Marathi : *ati sahana tyaca bayen rikama*

Bengali : *ati chalakra boka hay*
Extra smart are stupid.

Marathi : *eka hatane tali bajat nahi*
Bengali : *ek hathe tali baje na*
Can't clap with one palm
It takes two to quarrel.

Marathi : *donda bhadela*
Bengali : *dhoni aro dhoni hote chay*
Rich want to become richer.

Marathi : *mana raja mana praja*
Bengali : *monyi raja monyi praja*
Mind is king and subject.

Marathi : *anganavaruna gharki kala*
Bengali : *uthan dekhe ghar bojha yay*
Courtyard speaks of the room
Morning shows the day.

**Punjabi**

In Punjabi also the proverb is *kahabat.*

Punjabi : *panjab de jawan te sher de santan ik brebar*
Bengali : *panjaber yubak singher bachcha*
Punjabi youth is a lion cub.

Punjabi : *kacci sone di paccahi*
Bengali : *noditirer jomi yena sonar khoni*
Land by the river is a gold mine.

Punjabi : *jo garje so bhasda nahin*
Bengali : *yata garje tata barshe na*
Rain does not match the thunder.

Punjabi : *golla hoke kamak, raja hoke khaye*
Bengali : *ye daser mato kaj kare se rajar mato khay*
He who toils like a slave eats like a king.

Punjabi : *jitni godi itni dodi*

Bengali : *yata chash tata phal*
More the farming more the yield.

Punjabi : *shakhna bhanda bahun kharkhe*

Bengali : *shunya kalsir aoaj beshi*
Empty vessel sounds the most.

Punjabi : *ik gandi macchahi sare jai nu ganda kar di hay*

Bengali : *dushta gorur chey shunya goal bhalo*
Empty cowshed better than a mischievous cow.

Punjabi : *ag bina dhun kitthe*

Bengali : *agun bina dhnoa britha*
Smoke without fire is useless.

Punjabi : *dur de dhol suhavene*

Bengali : *durer shabda modhur hay*
Noise from far is sweet
Distant pastures are greener.

**Gujarati**

Proverb is *kahewat.*

Gujarati : *jebu babo tedhu lono*

Bengali : *yeman karma teman phal*
Reap as you sow.

Gujarati : *dubto manas tankhanlu pabade*

Bengali : *dubanta manush khadrkuto dhore banche chay*
Drowing man wants to catch at any straw.

Gujarati : *dungara durathi raliamana*

Bengali : *durer pahada sundar dekhay*
Distant hills (pastures) are greener.

Gujarati : *dudhno dajhelo chash phunkeene peebe*

Bengali : *ghar poda goru sindure megh dekhle bhay pay*

Cow that has known fire fears the red cloud.

Gujarati : *jeba sathe teba*
Bengali : *dhil chhundle patkelti khete hay*
Tit for tat.

Gujarati : *dheerjanan phal mithang*
Bengali : *sabure meoa phale*
Patience yields fruits.

Gujarati : *hawa man killa bhandba*
Bengali : *akash kusum kalpana kara*
Building castles in the air.

Gujarati : *mon hoy ta malbe jabay*
Bengali : *ichchha thakle upay hay*
Where there is a will there is a way.

Gujarati : *ati lobh se papnun mool*
Bengali : *ati lobhe tanti nashta*
Too much greed kills.

Gujarati : *cheenma cha becba jabun*
Bengali : *tela mathay tel deoa*
Greasing oiled palms
Carrying coal to Newcastle.

Gujarati : *khale ane darbaja mokle*
Bengali : *ek paisar janya karpanya, anyadike taka kharach*
Penny wise pound foolish.

Gujarati : *chore chore masiai bhai*
Bengali : *chore chore mastuto bhai*
Thieves are cousins under the skin.

Gujarati : *jhajhee suralee bastar bethe*
Bengali : *adhik sanyasite gajan nashta*
Too many cooks spoil the broth.

Gujarati : *kheela chano bage ghono*

Bengali : *shunya kalsir aoaj beshi*

Empty vessel sounds the most

Gujarati : *ek hathe tali na pade*

Bengali : *ek hate tali baje na*

Can't clap with one palm

It takes too to quarrel.

## Rajasthani

*Okhani* or *kahabat* is the Rajasthani for proverb.

Rajasthani : *jobnia tun bhalan hee jajye tumat jajye taharka*

Bengali : *youban kshanasthayi*
*roop chirasthayi*

Youth is fleeting, beauty everlasting.

Rajasthani : *kali kayan hee theeke ar gori kayan hee theeke*

Bengali : *sundar mukher jay sarbatra*

Beauty triumphs everywhere.

Rajasthani : *ek ke dand se sou ke sabhai bhal*

Bengali : *swalpe labhe punji bade*

Slow and steady wins the race.

Rajasthani : *baman hathi chadon bhi mang*

Bengali : *baman hathi chadleo bhiksha kare*

Dwarf begs even from elephant back

Habits die hard.

Rajasthani : *ammar racyo meh macyo*

Bengali : *sindure megh brishtir lakshman*

Scarlet cloud indicates rain (Sign of danger).

## Kashmiri

In the 'Koser' language of Kashmir, the proverb is again called, *kahabat.*

Kashmiri : *chheli chheli zun z filum*

Bengali : *dushter motigoti bojha mushkil*

Hard to understand ways of the bad.

Kashmiri : *dana dushman chui nadan netharah sandih khutak jan*

Bengali : *murkha bondhur cheye bignya shatru bhalo*

Wise foe is better than a stupied friend.

Kashmiri : *gabih buthih rumah-hun*

Bengali : *bhedar chhadmabeshe nekde*

Wolf in sheep's clothing.

Kashmiri : *namedanam chui rahat-i-janam*

Bengali : *agnata shanti*

Ignorance is bliss.

Kashmiri : *sheth gav zih braeth gav*

Bengali : *shat bachar hole boka hay*

makes seven years a stupid.

Kashmiri : *sumur nai sunah tsir karih tah kats gatshes*

Bengali : *swarnakar mayer gahano churi kare*

Goldsmith steals even mother's ornaments.

**Konkani**

Konkani : *anna paileng peet subbay paileng meet*

Bengali : *durer jinis maricika*

Thing far off is a mirage.

Konkani : *jabyank dillelen rebentu muttilen sama*

Bengali : *jamai sab samay hat pate*

Son-in-law is ever demanding.

Konkani : *gharat ghyalari pikna, anganti rhelyari bikna*

Bengali : *makal phale kono kaj hay na*

Looks serve no purpose.

### Parsi

Parsi : *akuilan peyarabhi ai tanukat na kunand*
Bengali : *bidyaner kono paricay lage na*
Learned needs no introduction.

Parsi : *cosham-i-ma raushan dil-i-ma khush*
Bengali : *chokher alo moner alo*
Eye's light, mind's light.

Parsi : *ebhaj mabhaj gila na darad*
Bengali : *gatasya shochana nasti*
Don't cry over spilt milk.

### Chakma

The Chakmas are tribals living in the Chittagong Hills of Bangladesh as also in some North-Eastern states of India. The proverb is known as *damarkada* and it has enriched the Chakma language.

Chakma : *nabit dele nakkuni bare*
Bengali : *napit dekhle nakher kona bade*
Finger nails grow at sight of barber.

Chakma : *ah libe kajya najha*
Bengali : *abahelay karya nashta*
Neglect spoils the work.

Chakma : *ghangda bhidire kangda*
Bengali : *ghomtar bhitare khemta*
Naughty under cover

Chakma : *sad ajhay pua marey*
Bengali : *adhik sannyasite gajan nashta*
Too many cooks spoil the broth.

Chakma : *ek tule khede*
*ek tule pude*
Bengali : *chasir kshet ar put sambal*
Farmer has only land and son to depend on.

Chakma : *duksh khar rait na phuray*
Bengali : *duksher rater shesh nei*
Misery knows no end.

Chakma : *ek to yay*
*lecchan thay*
Bengali : *din yay katha thake*
Time passes word stays.

Chakma : *dur a kudum phul bas*
*kay a kudum cinda bas*
Bengali : *durer kutum phuler bas*
*kacher kutum chimse bas*
Distant relation smells of flower, near one stinks
Familiarity breeds contempt.

Chakma : *par a kadat ksn na day*
*alpa khea sajag rya*
Bengali : *parer kathay kan deo na*
*alpa kheye santushta thako*
Be satisfied with what you have.

Chakma : *gojen yadi koi dey*
*gharat ani boi dey*
Bengali : *gojen yadi icchha karen*
*ghare ese pounchhe dyan*
God takes care of the fortunate.

Chakma : *ye kukurer lej benga*
*cumat bharileo ujna na hay*
Bengali : *ye kukurer lej byanka*
*hajar chumuteo soja habe na*
Can't straighten a dog's tail.

Chakma : *cura nange cur thay*
*bainga nane cur thay*
Bengali : *shakunir chokh padarer dike*
Vulture's eye fixed on garbage dump.

**Jharkhand Tribals (JT)**

JT : *budhal na baunal*
Bengali : *teen matha yar, buddhi nebe tar*

Consult him with three heads

Consult the old (three heads mean the actual head and the two knees on both sides as he squats on the ground).

JT : *lodi dhare chas, micha kara ash*

Bengali : *nodir dhare chash kara ar dhaner asha kara mithya*

Farm by the river, expect no crop.

JT : dhol *bajabi paysa libi*

Bengali : *phelo kodi macho tel*

Pay and take.

JT : *ek hate madal baje na*

Bengali : *ek hate tali baje na*

It takes two to tango (to quarrel).

JT : kan tanlei mudh ase

Bengali : *kan tanle matha ase*

Pull the ear and head will come.

JT : *ada ante mudi phank*

Bengali : *nun ante panta phuray*

Hand to mouth.

JT : *lodha paday labanga bikri*

Bengali : *ulu bane chash*

Selling spectacles to the blind.

**Santhali**

Proverb is *men katha* in Santhali and sayings, *venta katha.*

Santhali : *ak lekam yera ana lekam ira*

Bengali : *yeman karma teman phal*

You reap as you sow.

Santhali : *al khan da thutige saresa*

Bengali : *lekhar theke shruti bhalo*

Listening is better than writing.

Santhali : *cetan rang chang, bhitri ondarbhang*
Bengali : *chakchak korlei sona hay na*
All that glitters is not gold.

Santhali : *janumate janum ge so hoyoh a*
Bengali : *kanta diye kanta tola*
Use a thorn to remove a thorn.

Santhali : *eken thili da sadegeya*
Bengali : *khepra dhenkir shabda beshi*
Empty vessel sounds most.

Santhali : *kanda hapa da mit chatgoy ada*
Bengali : *neda ekbari beltalay yay*
Don't repeat mistake.

Santhali : *dhinki butam senah rese loboh khadem jama*
Bengali : *kashta na korle keshta mele na*
No fruits without labour.

Santhali : *sahao khanem lahah a*
Bengali : *ye sahe se rahe*
Lives he who suffers.

**Rajbansi**

In the Rajbansi language of North Bengal, the proverb is known both as *siluk* and *conok*

Rajbansi : *kauar bhasat kokiler chao, jat sobhabe kare ao*
Bengali : *kaker basay kokiler chha, yar chha tar ra*
Cuckoo chick in crow's nest, her chicks not her own.

Rajbansi : *khay day pakhi baner viti ankhi*
Bengali : *khanchar pakhi akashe udte chay*
Caged bird longs the sky.

Rajbansi : *ye din maribe hari ki korbo dang nadi*
Bengali : *mrityu kauke kshama kare na*
Death spares none.

Rajbansi : *hal nai hatiar nai langtia sepai*

Bengali : *dhal nei tolowar nei, nidhiram sardar*
Soldier sans arms is a joke.

Rajbansi : *kharkhar nari, jharjhar jhari*
*chor nafar parapara ghar*
*tak hati durat sar*

Bengali : *asati nari, phuto kalsi, asat chakar, bhagnapray badi. Parityajjya*

Avoid unchaste woman, leaking pitcher, dishonest servant, crumbling house.

Some regional variations of the same proverb:

(1) Bad workman blames his tools :
*Nachte na janle uthan byanka* (Bengali)
*nach na jane angan tera* (Urdu)
*chali na jani batar dosh* (Oriya)
*nacat eyina angan bhokra* (Marathi)
*kunyialike tenia diddake angar orey* (Kannad)

(2) Honey-tongued, venom inside :
*mukhe madhu antare bish* (Bengali)
*mukhme mitha dil se jahar* (Hindi)
*bish kumbham poyomukham* (Oriya)
*uudttile uurbu nenjile pahai* (Tamil)
*bai illadi sihi mannavalli kahi* (Kannada)

(3) It takes two to quarrel :
*ek hat tali baje na* (Bengali)
*ek hath se tali nahi bajat* (Hindi)
*gote hathe tali baje nahi* (Oriya)
*ek hatale tali bajat nahi* (Marathi)
*ek hate tali na pade* (Gujarati)
*mit dharate pitha da ban isinah a* (Santhali)

(4) All that glitters is not gold :
*chakchak karlei sona hay na* (Bengali)
*chakchak marlei sona nahi* (Oriya)
*holey yuvudhela holalla* (Kannada)
*minudellam ponnalla* (Malayalam)
*cetan rang chang bhitri ondarbhang* (Santhali)

(5) Empty vessel sounds the most :
*shunya kalsir aoaj beshi* (Bengali)
*shakhna bhanda bahuun kharkhe* (Punjabi)
*khali chano bage ghano* (Gujarati)

(6) Too many cooks spoil the broth :
*adhik sanyasite gajan nashta* (Bengali)
*jhajhi surani bantar betho* (Gujarati)
*sad ajhay pua marey* (Chakma)

(7) Excessive greed kills :
*ati lobhe tanti nashta* (Bengali)
ati lobh se papnum mool (Gujarati)

(8) Tit for tat : *Dhil chundle patkel khate hay* (Bengali)
*jeba sathe teba* (Gujarati)

(9) Distant pastures are greener :
*Durer pahad sundar dekhay* (Bengali)
*dur pahad sundar* (Oriya)
*dungara durathee raliamana* (Gujarati)

(10) Pot calling the kettle black:

*chhunch bale chalunike tor pichhane kena phuto* (Bengali)

*chluni kahe chhucan ki, to pachhare gotie kana* (Oriya)

(11) Carrying coal to Newcastle:
*tela mathay tel deoa* (Bengali)
*ceenman ca bejba jobun* (Gujarati)

Given below are some Bengali proverbs with their foreign counterparts:

English : *thonta mukh bhonta haoa*

To make a sharp knife blunt.

*ye chale se rahe*

Rolling stone gathers no moss.

*nei mamar ceye kana mama bhalo*

Half a loaf is better than no bread.

*chanchalata nashter mool*

Haste makes waste.

*ek hate tali baje na*

It takes two to quarrel.

*durbhagya ekla ase na*

Misfortune never comes singly.

*arthai shakti*

Money is power.

*artha anarther mool*

Money is at the root of all trouble.

*ati ghanishta bhalo nay*

Familiarity breeds contempt.

American : *shamuker matan nirbak*

Dumb as an oyster.

Bengali : *chor palale buddhi bade*

Arabic : Yazda all aqlu bada farar issariq.

Some examples of the same proverb in different languages:

(1) nei mamar ceye kana mama bhalo (Bengali)
Half a loaf is better than no bread (English)
*ek bhi mama na none se kana mama ta accha hai* (Hindi)
Lieber etwas als nichts (German)
Sparrow in hand is better than crane in air (Persian)
Bird in cage is worth a bird at large (Italian)

(2) *tela mathay tel deoa* (Bengali)
To carry coal to Newcastle (English)
*soney pad suhaga caran* (Hindi)
To pour water into Severn (Welsh)
To carry apples to Aleinous (Greek)
To carry leaves to the wood (American)
To carry peppers to Hindustan (Persian)

(3) *deoaler kan ache* (Bengali)
Walls have ears (English)
Die waude haben dharen (German)
A falnak pule van (Hungarian)
Er shu yu yain (Chinese)
kabi ni mini (ari) (Japanese)

(4) *mukhe madhu hride bish* (Bengali)
A honey tongue, a heart of gall (English)
*mukh me ram bagal me churi* (Hindi)
Mel in ore, fel in corde (Latin)
Honig im munde und ga Galle im Herzen (German)
kumilpokkam (Korean)

(5) *yeman manib teman chakar* (Bengali)
Like master, like man (English)
*yatha raja tatha praja* (Hindi)
Qalis dominus, toils of servus (Latin)
Wie der Herr, so's Gescherr (German)

(6) *ulu vane mukto charano* (Bengali)
Casting pearls before the swine (English)
*andho ke shahar me aina becna* (Hindi)
Man soll die perlen nicht vor die saue werfen (German)

(7) *Samay eban kaler srot karur janya apeksha kare na* (Bengali)
Time and tide waits for none (English)
*waqt kisi ka intejar nahi karta* (Hindi)
die zeit warter auf nienand (German)
Saigetsu hito wo matazi (Japanese)

(8) *ek hate tali baje na* (Bengali)
It takes two to quarrel (English)
kosho marashi gatashi (Japanese)
*ek hat se tali nahi bajti* (Hindi)
*ek hatane tali bajat nahee* (Marathi)

(9) *akash kusum* (Bengali)
Building castles in the air (English)
*haoa me phool bandhna* (Hindi)
Luftschosser bauen (German)

(10) *ek dhile dui pakhi* (Bengali)
Killing two birds with one stone (English)
Zwei fliegen mit einer klappe (German)

(11) *gharpoda goru sindure megh dekhle bhay pay* (Bengali)
Bird once wounded is afraid of the bow (English)
dudh ka jal chhachh bhi phunk kar pita hoi (Hindi)
Jin shu-shinjo (Chinese)
Sanggungchi jo kydong kingmokira (Korean)
Shokyu no tori wa kyochatsu ni otsu (Japanese)

(12) *chore chore mastuto bhai* (Bengali)
Set a thief to catch a thief (English)
*chor chor mousere bhai* (Hindi)
Like attracts like (English)

(13) *sab samayer shesh achhe* (Bengali)
Every flow has its ebb (English)
haar samayka ant hota hoi (Hindi)
Jede Flut hat ibre Ebbe (German)
Minden husvetnak van bojtje (Hungarian)

(14) *ekta kukur chenchale sahasra kukur chenchay* (Bengali)
If a dog barks at a shadow, a hundred will bark loudly (English)
ek kutta bhukne se sab kutta bhukte hoi (Hindi)
ein narr macht hunder/viel narren (German)
One fool makes many (English)
Egy bolond szazat csinal (Hungarian)

Such similar proverbs could have come into being naturally because of similarities of experience or these could have found their way to different languages as communication between people grew. The contact could have been through the peaceful process of trade and commerce or through war and territorial occupation. Such were the ways in which people living along the Mediterranean came in touch with those in Asia Minor, India and China. This is what is known as 'acculturation' and reminds one of the Bengali proverb, *sahasra baran gavire bhai, ek baran dudh*—cows have many colours but their milk has only one.

# 9

# Conclusion

What transpires from our discussions in the preceding chapters is the fact that of all forms of folk literature it is the proverb which is closest to life and hence the most popular. This is true for proverbs all over the world. Being a part of the oral tradition it can be safely assumed that the proverb will remain as long as human civilization exists and of all elements of folklore it enjoys the greatest practical value. The question is, why?

Based on tradition, these simple yet bright utterances are a means of guiding mankind along the correct path and so are both ancient and contemporary. There is no subject in man's world of both thought and action that has not been covered by proverbs or popular sayings which are a loose form of the proverb. So proverbs abound in the thousand-year old Bengali literature, from the writings of Sarhapa (*charyageeti)* to the poets of today.

The life of a people is reflected in art and literature and an analysis of about ten thousand proverbs shows that the proverbs of Bengal have captured life in its totality. From farming to social relations, environment protection to public health, issues related to caste, economic disparity, there are proverbs for every occasion. Together they constitute folk literature about which Tagore had said, "literature for all times formed by piecing together the disjointed everyday activities in the villages, the making of the plough, the *dhenki,* the gold ornaments".[1]

The first duty of a patriot is to know his own country, particularly its culture which expresses people's desires and aspirations. In our country the initiative in this was first taken by foreign scholars; the unfortunate history of the $19^{th}$ century educated Bengali ignoring his own cultural tradition is well known. So during the agitation against the partition of Bengal in 1905, Tagore had regretted, "nothing can be more shameful than our indifference to our own country, we fail to realize that this is an abuse that we are showering on ourselves".[2] This indifference towards folk culture continued even in later years, causing Dr. Sushil Kumar De to remark, "in the modern cultured society, the proverbs may not be directly criticized but they are ignored".[3]

The reason, as he found out, was that the Western educated Bengalis found these to be nothing but rustic and often obscene sayings, even though Tagore had made the strong statement that these components of Bengali language and literature could not be kept aside if a complete picture of the nation was to be got. He wrote, "You do not have the right to ignore, you do not have the right to call it insignificant, you cannot turn up your nose at the language dubbing it as 'slang'. If you do that then you yourself will become an object of pity. I shall not use a stronger word".[4]

With all his interest in folk culture, Tagore, however, did not show any great interest in the proverb, perhaps because others had done so before him. At the same time he had recognized the importance of the proverb as one of the elements of folk literature. This he made clear in an essay which appeared in *Sadhana,* the Sahitya Parishad journal, in 1301 of the Bengali calendar. He wrote, "the journal should shoulder the responsibility of collecting the folklore of Bengal, the proverbs and sayings, nursery rhymes".

The poet succeeded in inspiring others and men like Aghore Nath Chattopadhyay and Dakshinaranjan Mitra Mazumdar devoted considerable time collecting fairy tales and the rhymes related to women's rituals or *brata.* In 1305 it was Madhumadhab Chattopadhyay's *Prabad Padmini,* a collection of proverbs in three volumes. Articles on proverbs also appeared in journals and such interest in the subject perhaps would not have been evinced but for Rabindranath Tagore.

## II

The work of collecting proverbs continued throughout the 19th and 20th centuries. We have already seen how these reflect traditional Bengali life. Now let us see the role of the proverb in modern urban society. Particularly the relevance of the agriculture related proverbs in the context of the present day concern for the environment. It is seen that such concern had been expressed through the proverbs long before modern man woke up to the dangers confronting the environment and thereby mankind as a whole. How long ago was it that Khana had said, *bon thakle brishti habey* or it will rain only if there are forests which is exactly what is being said in the contemporary stress on forest cover. Today it has almost become a fashion to go for walks in the morning but do the walkers know that in the hoary past there was a Bengali saying, *berao yadi bhorer bela/thakbe na are roger jvala*—if you take a walk in the morning, you will not suffer from illness.

The proverbs are also valuable source material for those engaged in Subaltern studies, Womens Studies, the proverbs on personalities like Mahipal, Rani Bhabani, Chand Roy, Kedar Roy, Nawab Asafuddouulah of Oudh can be of immense help to those recreating regional history. Today everybody, including the government, is concerned at the killing of female foetus but they could have been aware of the menace if they had paid any attention to the ancient proverbs. Such killings are the result of the age old belief that the daughter was a burden, a belief born out of social conditions, and the proverbs like, *sat janme pap korli meye janme tabe eli,* born a daughter because of sins in past seven lives. If the world had not turned a blind eye to such proverbs then measures perhaps could have been taken to prevent what is happening today. At the same time it is in proverbs that today's social scientist can find instances of female protest, like in *bhat dey na bhatare / bhat dey gatare,* it is not the husband who feeds, it is my physical labour that does. As for those seeking to uphold women's rights, the gigantic nature of their task is made clear by the proverbs of yore which reflect the way society continued to maltreat women throughout the ages. The examples provided already by the proverbs on the dowry system, bride burning, torture of wives in general and the attitude towards women's education, illustrate the point.

Social scientists can always turn to these proverbs to support the justified contention that working people in this country, as also elsewhere, have always been victims of oppression. Those like, *chaser duksha egaro mas* (peasant suffers eleven months a year) or *khete khaoa yader barat / tader katbe na dukher rat* (the night of misery will ever end for those whose lot it is to toil) were not born out of somebody's imagination, these were products of prevailing social conditions. That society has always been governed by commerce is evident from proverbs like, *korite miley bagher dudh* or money can fetch even tiger's milk. And the realization of the essential nature of city life remains valid even today—*mithya kathar kiba keta / ajab shahar koliketa* meaning strange is the city of Kolkata where lies are told in so many ways.

The relevance of these proverbs in today's life does not just end there. A nation plagued by ills like communalism needs messages conveyed by proverbs like, *ram, rahim, kali / bhed korlei moli* or separate Ram, Rahim, Kali and perish. In a discussion on folk literature at Santiniketan, Tagore had said, "if a comparative analysis is made of nursery rhymes of different parts of India then that will be very educational as it will show the capture the basic similarity among the different races in the country".[5] This has been seen to be true by an analysis of proverbs also. How correct was the late President K.R. Narayanan when he said, "Indian literature is one, only published in different languages". An instance of a proverb can be taken : a bad workman blames his tools the Bengal version being, *nachte na janle uthan byanka* or can't dance and blames the floor. Exactly the same proverb is found in Urdu, Hindi, Oriya, Marathi and in the language of Karnataka, the difference being only linguistic. This has already been discussed and a comparative study or proverbs of other countries has been made to show that a common thread ties not only different linguistic groups within a country but all over the world. This is the kind of globalization that is desired by all right thinking people.

As said already, the language of the Bengali proverb is the everyday language of the ordinary people, a language which till recently was looked down upon. But today, as Tagore had said would happen, it has got its rightful place by shaving aside the Sanskritised Bengal understandable only to the few.

The danger, however, of this natural language being attacked remains. The post-second war neo-colonialist exploitation manifests itself both in the economic and cultural sphere and as a nation of the third world, we have not been left unaffected. Not just the urban centres, thanks to technological innovations even the rural areas are today victims of a perverse culture in the spread of which the mass media is playing a big role. From early morning the FM channel brings a strange cocktail of English, Hindi and Bengali, traditional eateries have been taken over by 'fast food joints', Valentine's Day has largely taken over the observance of age old rituals and Bengali literature is represented by pulp fiction. The country has become the happy hunting ground of a set of rootless people without any awareness of values, our identity is under threat. Eminent leaders throughout the world are worried at this and the words of Fidel Castro are worth recalling:

"It is not a world order that combines the wealth and culture of many countries but a world order that, by definition, destroys culture, a globalization that inevitably destroys culture.

"What is one's homeland, if not one's culture? What is national identity if not the country's own culture? Can there be a greater spiritual wealth then one's own culture, created during eons by mankind, can our customs be simply swept away, ruthlessly swept away? We have to be aware of that, because the battles of ideas and concepts will be a great battle". (*Fidel Castro: Neoliberal Globalization and the Global Economic Crisis,* NBA Private Limited, 1999, p. 124).

A way out of this crisis is the protection of our own cultural heritage. The people have to be made to look inwards, to re-discover themselves. And that re-discovery will not be possible without taking note of the rich folk culture of which the proverbs and sayings are an integral part. No conscious individual, no matter how modern he may be in his outlook, can tear himself away from his roots of which proverbs are an eloquent symbol. Thus in his Goopi Gyne Bagha Byne, Satyajit Ray composed the famous song the theme of which was the age old proverb, *pete khele pithe shay* or a filled tummy can bear the beating and the post-modern singer made good use of the saying, *tak thakle taka hay* meaning a bald head and money go together. This is not necessarily true but it was used cleverly to ridicule a consumerist society. Thus has the proverb lived through the ages and so is it called a permanent treasure in human civilization. If a people allow proverbs to die then they will also bring about their own downfall. It is hoped that Bengal will renew its heritage and proverbs as well as other components of our indigenous literature will continue to enjoy their well earned space in life.

## References

1. Tagore, Rabindranath, Rabindra Rachanavali, Centenary Vol., Part XIII, p. 717.
2. Tagore, Rabindranath, Rabindra Rachanavali, Centenary Vol., Part XIII, p. 876.
3. De, Sushil Kumar, Banglar Probad, 1408, Introduction, p. 25.
4. Tagore, Rabindranath, Rabindra Rachanavali, Centenary Vol. XIII, p. 788.
5. Ashram Sambad, Santiniketan Patrika, Chaitra, 1328, p. 39.

# APPENDIX–A
## Field Survey

Some of the proverbs collected from residents of villages in West Bengal and Bangladesh along with their names and addresses.

**24-Parganas (North)**

Village Sandeshkhali, resident Anima Das (50), teacher:

*jor yar mulluk tar*
World belongs to the strong.
*taka nebe gune, path chalbe jene*
Count your money, know your path.
*chor palale buddhi bade*
Wise after the event
Bolting the stable after the horse has fled.
*gaye mane na apni modal*
Self proclaimed leader.
*sharirer nam mahashay, ya soabe tai say*
Body adapts to everything.
*bansher cheye konchi dada*
Reed stronger than the bamboo.

**24-Parganas (South)**

Village Kumarimari, resident Padma Dasi (58) housewife:

*agachhar gachh beshi, akamer katha beshi*
Empty vessel sounds the most.
*yadi dekho makunda dhopa*
*badao na ek pa bapa*
Beware of the hairless.
*adhik sanyasite gajan nashta*

Too many cooks spoil the broth.

*apni banchle baper nam*

Self comes first.

**Howrah**

Village Bankurda, resident Suren Kar (50) farmer;

*kayeter mada bhase*
*kak boley kon chale hase*

Kayastha is never to be trusted.

*ati bado sundari na pay bar*

Looks alone don't help.

**Hooghly**

Village, Balarampur, resident Bibhuti Roy (78), teacher;

*pet khasale pap, pete dhorle shap*

Sin if aborted, cursed if not.

*saper hanchi bedey chene*

It takes a wook to know another.

*tenar hal nai*
*unar balad nai*

One has no plough, the other no bullock

**Burdwan**

Village Nischintipur, resident Mahamaya Roy (72), housewife:

*alpa shoke kator/adhik shoke pathor*

Small sorrows disturb, major one turns speechless.

*aam, amda, kajda dhan/tin niye bardhaman*

Mangoe, hog-plum, paddy, three make Bardhaman

*yeman kukur teman mugur*

As is the dog so is the club.

*chhoonch churi korte kudul haray*

Stealing needle, losing the axe (Penny wise, pound foolish).

*jait gyalo, pet bharlo na*

Become outcaste, yet stay hungry (Risking to no avail).

**Birbhum**

Village Kaleswar, resident, Nityanarayan Bhattacharya (52), teacher:

*ek anchadey bojha yay*

One scratch tells everything (Morning shows the day).

*swabhab yay na mole*

Habits die hard.

*artha anarther mool*

Money is the root of all trouble.

*uchit kathay manush hoy rushta, devata santushta*

Just word angers man, pleases god.

*ek kadar murod nei, bhat marar gosain*

Not worth a dime, talking big.

**Midnapore**

Village Lalgar, resident Shyamal Maity (55), teacher:

*nachte na janle uthaner dosh*

Can't dance, blames the floor (Bad workman blames his tools).

*kana chheler nam padmalochan*

Blind son named Lotus-eye

*anabhasyer phonta chadchad kare*

Undeserved honour hurts.

*ek kan diye shone, anyakan diye bar kore*

Enters through one ear, goes out the other.

**Bankura**

Village Sonamukhi, resident Saswati Mandal (45), teacher:

*banja ki bujhbek pasab yatana*

What does the barren know of birth pangs?

*pete bhat nai, paye alta*

Empty stomach, lac-dye on feet.

*rajay kare pap, proja pay tap*

King sins subjects suffer.

*maga bhat tay basi a panta*

Got rice begging, ask not whether stale or watered (Don't look a gift horse in the mouth).

**Nadia**

Village Anandapalli, resident Swapna Bhattacharya (57), housewife:

*aage tita pichha mitha*

Bitter first sweet later.

*ude ese jude basa*

Coming in from nowhere and occupying.

*ek yatray prithak phal*

Same mission, different result.

*kukurer pete ghee say na*

Butter does not suit dogs.

*jale bas kore kumirer sange bibad*

Living in water, fighting with crocodile

**Murshidabad**

Village Nabagram, resident Parul Ghosh (50), housewife:

*ek hate tali baje na*

No one can clap with one palm.

*icchha thakle upay hay*

Where there is a will there is a way.

*ek kil diye eksha kil khay*

Gives one and gets hundred back.

*achhe goru na bay hal, tar duksha chirakal*

His suffering does not end whose ox does not work.

*jahuri na hole jahar chinte pare na*

It takes a jeweller to know jewels.

**Malda**

Village Ratua, resident Bishnucharan Majhi (60), agriculturist:

*phuler ghaye murchha yay*

Faints at flower's touch.

*pagole ki na bale chhagale ki na khay*

Lunatic's words and goat's food.

*dhori machh na chhuin pani*

Catch fish but don't get wet.

*dashir katha basi hole mishti lagey*

Maid's words are sweet when stale. (when they prove right in the end).

*dant thakte danter marma bujhi na*

Tooth's worth unknown while there.

*jeevan, youban gele ar phere na*

Life and youth never come back.

*ratanei rattan chene*

Takes a crook to know another.

*hater phank diye jal gale na*

Water does not pass through (his) fingers (A miser).

**Jalpaiguri/Cooch Behar**

Village Jalpesh, Jalpaiguri, resident Smriti Gangopadhyay (56), housewife:

*patiheen youban*
*sajgoj akaran*

Youth without husband
Pointless to dress.

*garam bhatey na khai ada*
*sipaiak na koi dada*

Don't need ginger with hot rice
Don't call the sepoy elder brother.
*par ki apan hay*
*shimule ki chandan hay*
Outsider does not become own
Sandalwood does not grow on Sheemul tree.
*dui naoey dia pao*
Keeping feet in two boats (Not committing himself).
*mukhe til muchuk hasi*
*sei nari parpurashi*
Dark spot on face, sly smile
that woman is no good.

**Darjeeling**

Village Chtodomgach, resident Parmila Singha (25), tea garden labourer:

*satloker bhater abhab hay na*
An honest man does not starve.
*yar katha ek, swargey martey thek*
Man of one word has place in earth and heaven.
*ghar poda goru dinat chamkay*
He who has suffered is ever alert.
*ghama masi*
One side good, other bad.
*tyaji thakurer bhiksha mai*
Anger makes good look bad.
*petpakhi*
To be jealous.
*angshang lagaye deshan*
At a loss for words.

**Bangladesh**

**Dhaka**

Village Paiti, resident Najid Hassan (52), agriculturist:

*ye yay lankay*
*she hay rakshas*

He who goes to Lanka
Becomes a demon
*yare dekhte nari*
*tar chalan banka*
His legs are wobbly
Whom I don't like
*yar nun khai*
*tar gun gai*
Praise him who feeds.
*sat puter maye bhikh mage*
*ek puter maye badshahi kare*
Mother of seven begs
Mother of one is a queen
*sati pay kul*
*asati pay kil*
Chaste gets shelter
naughty gets blows.

**Narayanganj**

Village Nabiganj, resident Raushan Ara (35), housewife:

*goborey padmaphool janme na*
Lotus does not grow in cowdung.
*dhenki swarge geleo dhan bhane*
Husking pedal husks paddy even in heaven (a toiler knows no rest).
*jater meye kalo bhalo*
*nadir jal ghola bhalo*
Dark girl of same caste good
river water, even dirty, good.
*Oti chalaker galay dodi*
Extra smart meets death.
*pradiper goday andhakar*
Darkness at base of lamp.

**Manikganj**

Village Sudhunagar, resident Makbul Chowdhury (42), teacher:

*chorer noukay sadhur nishan*

Thief's boat flies the saint's flag.
*sona thuiye anchale ginth*
Losing the gold fastening sari end
(Bolting the stable after horse has fled).
*kajar kay suinre, tor pachhay tera*
Pot calling the kettle black.
*anbar koichi langal, loia aiche gai*
Asked for plough brought the cow.
*yubati narir hay ananda babay yadi dyay bia*
*budo budir hay ananda nati natni paia*
Young girl fals happy when given in marriage
Old parents feel happy when grand children come.
*byang byangir hay ananda notun pani paia*
*petuker hay ananda parer badi khaia*
Frogs are happy to get new rain water
Gourmand happy eating at another's house.

**Faridpur**

Village Choumuk, resident Abdul Khalek (56), teacher:

*nijer machay thakli*
*sab cnacnar nagol paoa yay*
Stick to own ground, others will come.
*parer pithe bejay mithe*
Others' pies are sweeter (Distant pastures are greener).
*thakti delo na bhut kapad*
*morli debeney than kapad*
Neither food nor clothes when alive
When I die will give new cloth.
*ami kandi mar lage*
*ma kande nanger lage*
I weep for mother
mother weeps for lover.

**Jessore**

Village Hajarhati, resident Meena Begum (42), housewife:

*tela mathay sagalei tel dhale*
Everybody oils the oily head
(Carrying coal to Newcastle).
*garibir katha basi hole khate*
Poor man's words believed but late.
*ek maghe sheet yay na*
One swallow does not make a summer.
*khaoar samay gai*
*biobar samay bachhur*
Cow when it comes to eating
calf when it comes to delivering.
*punti machher paran*
Heart of a small fish, a coward.

**Khulna**

Village Fatehpur, resident Nurul Huda (45), teacher:

*baper badi mati, chupchupay hanti*
*shashur badir mati, dabdabay hanti*
Walk softly at father's home
Stamp around at in-laws' place.
*mar peter bhai*
*mere yay tabu phire chai*
Though brother beats I look for him.
*yekhane geli bagher bhay*
*sekhane geli rat hay*
Night comes where there is fear of tiger.
*kathay katha bade*
*bhojane bade pet*

Words lead to more words (and eating makes tummy bigger-the second line is actually only for purpose of rhyming).

**Kusthia**

Village Jagalba, resident Ruksana Begum (40), housewife:

*kam apna, bhat parer*
Do my work, think not of reward.
*chhoto chhoto kamade*
*sab bhat hamure*

Small bites finish the meal.

*kshet chhaday peti*
*put chhaday durgati*

Farm removes want
son removes troubles.

*hatey karo hater kam*
*mukhe allar nam*

Let hands do the work, mouth utter God's name.

**Comilla**

Village Ranabati, resident Lata Nayek (43), housewife:

*yar lagi korlam churi sei dake chor*

For whom I stole, has called me a thief.

*bujher dushman bhalo*
*be bujher dost bhalo na*

Intelligent enemy better than stupid friend.

*joyer kale kshay nai*
*marar kale ousadh nai*

No loss at moment of triumph
No medicine at time of death.

*chhotoloker bish hate / badoloker bish dante*

Poor carries poison in hand, rich in his teeth.

**Mymensingh**

Village Ghaghra, resident Parul Biswas (44), housewife:

*agayna pat chhade na*

Does not walk, does not give way (Dog in the manger).

*kapale achhe har, ki korbo chacha shahidar*

If defeat is ordained who can help?

*jhade bag mare phakirer keramati bade*

Storm kills bird, fakir claims success.

*thelat porle bageo dan khay*

When in trouble even tiger eats paddy.

*churer mane pulish pulish*

Thief only has police in mind.

**Kishoreganj**

Village Bagadia, resident Mohammed Saidur (65), researcher:

*rajay rajay yuddha hay*
*chunopuntir pran yay*
Kings battle, small fry die.
*kanar rat ki, din ki*
Blind has neither night nor day.
*nijey banchli babar nam*
Save yourself at first, then save others.
*mane ya kay*
*pone ta hay*
What the mind says, happens.

**Jamalpur**

Village Pakutia, resident Rehana Sultana (38), teacher:

*pete kshudha mukhey laj*
Hunger in tummy, mouth shy to say
*yar kaj tarey saje*
Right man for the right job.
*kali, kalam, mon, lekhe teenjan*
Ink, pen and mind are the three who write.
*shashur badi modhur hadi, dui din pare jhantar badi*
In-laws' place sweet but after two days comes the broom.
*hati garte podle chamchikeo lathi maare*
Elephant in hole, everybody kicks.
*yeman buno ol, teman bagha tentul*
As is the ailment so is the medicine.

**Pabna**

Village Hemayatpur, resident Sona Begum (35), Housewife:

*hatir nimijhimi, ghodar doud*

Elephant ambles, horse runs
*jhaal jabd ashili*
*bou jabda kili*
Grinding stone subdues chilli
Blows subdue wife.
*shudhu kathay chinde bheje na*
Mere words serve no purpose.
*dan hatkhan dili*
*bam hatkhan paoa yay*
Give the right hand, the left will come.
*dudher swad ghole mete na*
Buttermilk is not milk (Substitute isn't good enough).
*satsange swargabas*
*asatsange sarbanash*
Good company heavenly
bad company disastrous.

**Sirajganj**

Village Ghoshgati, resident Sirajul Islam (48), teacher:

*sada kapode dag lage beshi*
White cloth gets more soiled (clean image gets soiled easily).
*labhe loha bay*
*bini labhe tulo bay na*
For money carries iron
Free, not even cotton.
*sharirer nam mahashay*
*ya soao tai say*
Human body takes everything.

**Rajsahi**

Village Ghoraghata, resident Saifuddin Chowdhury (50), teacher:

*yama, jamai, jamidar*
*teen nay apnar*
Yama, son-in-law, landlord, three are never yours.
*bokar phasal pokay khay*

Insects eat stupid man's crop.

*adhik lobhe tanti nashta*

Excess greed kills the weaver.

*chorer badi dalan uthe na*

Thief does not build big house.

**Sunamganj**

Village Dhanaidaha, resident Tapan Barik (38), agriculturist:

*pan, pani, nari, teene jaintapuri*

Betel leaf, water, women, three make Jaintapuri.

*maye jhi, gaie ghee, bape beta, gachhe gota*

Mother gives daughter, cow ghee, father gives son, tree gives fruit.

*aagc khatta pichhe dail*

Sour first, pulses later.

*chhatki chun, jaintapuri pan*

chhirimangaler cha-pata, hachhan rajar gan

Lime of Chatak, betel leaf or Jaintapuri tea of Srimangal, song of Hasan raja.

*Kuay thaki ailo umanya beta*
*he pailo maugya bata*
*ar ami ye chachar ghare bhai*
*amar lagi maug nai*

Comes frog from the well
he gets a wife
I her uncle's son
No wife for me.

**Gopalganj**

Village Tajpur, resident Lachman Molla (58), agriculturist:

*ghughu dyakcho ghughur phand dyakho nai*

Seen the bird, not the trap.

*bojhar upar shager anti*

Bunch of creepers on the huge load (Last straw on the camel's back).

*lebu anek chipraley tento hay*
Excess sqeazing turns lemon bitter.
*darogar cheye darogar majhir chot beshi*
Hireling shouts more than his boss.
*dharmer janya deenata, prakash kare namrata*
Humility shows softness.

**Nilfamari**

Village Barabazar, resident Jyotiprakash Saha (48), teacher:

*chhaoa chine baap mon chine paap*
Father knows his son
Mind recognises sin.
*yaen kare parer aash*
*nitya kare upabas*
Who depends on others, starves.
*akalat na khay ki*
*jhagrat na kay ki*
What does not the goat eat
What is not said in a quarrel.
*mude maye randhe na*
*tapta aar panta*
Mother does not cook
so why ask hot or cold.
*napit dekhte kunir naukh baare*
Sight of barber makes nail grow.

**Joypurhat**

*kotoi dekhbo kotoi aar*
*bidaler galay chandrahar*
What more is there to see
cat wearing neck lace
*dekhte na parle hantan byanka*
Dislike a person, make fun of his walk.
*naker upar diye nouka gechhe*
Boat has gone over the nose.
*jamaier janya maare hans*
*sara badi khay mas*

Duck killed for son-in-law
everybody eats (finding an excuse for doing things).
*naame akash phaate*
*handi patil kuttay chatey*
His name makes the sky break
dogs to lick cooking pots (said about misers).

**Jhalakathi**

Village Mahasthan, resident Fakirdudin Shah (52), agriculturist:

*pay na pacha punti*
*khayte chay ghi ruti*
He, who does not get rotten fish,
wants buttered bread.
*bou bhalo bate*
*thokna khaia batna bate*
Wife is good
works when sold.
*Ghare nai ghatibati*
*bouyer kapale sinthipati*
No utensils at home
Jewellery on wife's head.
*Mar chaiya pode mashi*
Aunt more concerned than mother.

**Chuadanga**

Village Jagalba, resident Nabi Sheikh (48), agriculturist:

*yar biye tar khabar nai*
*para podshir ghum nai*
Bride unconcerned, neighbours losing sleep.
*nei kaj ta khoi bhaj*
No work then fry puffed rice (passing the time).
*bhat deyar bhatar na, kil marar gosain*
Husband can't feed but ready to beat.
*dhaan bhante bolle bou admoda bhange*

*ghate yete bolle yena teji ghoda chhote*

Asked to husk paddy wife pretends illness

Runs like a horse when asked to go the river (place for gossiping).

**Barisal**

Village Olania, resident Mihir Dutta, journalist:

*mayer paraney chhabir tyana, polay kare babuana*

Mother in rags, son finely dressed.

*ghar nai, guar dia hoy*

No house but shuts the door before sleeping (showing off).

*thyada takko*

Pointless argument.

*duidiner bairagi, bhatre kay parsadi*

Recent convert putting on holy airs.

*paysa diya khamu dai, goalini amar kiser soyi*

Shall l pay for the curd, what friendship with the milkmaid.

**Noakhali**

Village Kabilpur, resident Ratan Bakshi (45), teacher:

*hola nashta ande*

*maiya nashta ghate*

Son spoilt in market

Girl spoilt in bathing ghat.

*randhi badi yeba nari, purusher aage khay*

*bhara kalsir jal tar tarase shukay*

Woman who eats before the men

Has her pitcher full of water drying up.

*sap, shala, jamidar, teen nay apnar*

Snake, brother-in-law, landlord, three are never yours

**Bhola**

Village Belka, resident Reena Begum, needlework artist:

*yadi hay sujan, tentul patay nayjan*

If friends then nine on a tamarind leaf.
*sabure meoa phale*
Patience pays.
*manush abhasyer daas*
Man is a creature of habits.
*bado yadi hote chao, chhoto hao tabe*
Want to be big, be small (humble) first.
*guru ninay adhogati*
Master's criticism leads to fall.

**Sylhet**

Village Brindabanpur, resident Niamat Hossain (57), agriculturist:

*aij khay na raage*
*kail hakkaler aage*
He who does not eat today in anger
eats first tomorrow.
*na haler na beecher*
Neither here nor there.
*dhan jan joani*
*kachu patar pani*
Wealth, friends, youth
Like water drops on a leaf.
*dhane na hay, bachane daridra nay*
Rich not in wealth but words.
*dharmer jai, adharmer kshay*
Truth triumphs, lies don't
*yeman kukur teman mugur*
As is the dog, so is the club.

**Feni**

Village Tajpur, resident Rumi Begum (37), housewife:

*chore chore ali*
*ek chore bia kare*
*arek chorer hali*
Crooks team up
One weds another's sister-in-law (birds of a feather, flock together).

*ek gachher chhal arek gachhe lage na*

One's coat does not fit another.

*thelathlir gha*

*khoday raksha kar*

God save the crowded house.

*chorer barite dalan uthe na*

Thief does not build big house (does not attract attention)

**Chattogram**

Village Patia, resident Rohit Baruah (45), teacher:

*kuar byeng sayarer khabar jane na*

Frog in well knows not about the sea.

*bandir kame yash nai*

*panta bhate kash nai*

No merit in maid's work

No fun in watered rice.

*bar angul kankduler tera angul guda*

Seed bigger than the fruit.

*ati adare baoas anadare sarbanash*

Too much care spoils, neglect causes disaster.

*ghar jamai bandir poot*

Resident son-in-law is the maid's son (Disliked by all).

*baap ma pay na bhat, amra phul hunkbar jaat*

Can't feed parents, spends time smelling flowers.

# APPENDIX-B
## Parts of Proverbs Collected by Rabindranath Tagore and Other Important Books

Rabindranath Tagore was one of the pioneers in the field of promoting folk literature and collecting samples pertaining to it. Towards the end of his life, in 1938, when writing *Bangla Bhasha Parichay,* he realized the importance of phrases in the proverbs and began compiling these. Given below are some examples:

*ga jvala kare*

Body has a burning sensation (out of anger, irritation)

*buk judie yay*

Heart is cooled (to be happy).

*tulo dhuno deoa*

Shredding cotton (to give a good shake up).

*paday paday teetee kora*

To defame in the neighbourhood.

*buddhir dhenki*

Mind's husking pedal (stupid).

*dharmaputtur yudhistir*

Yudhistir, son of Dharma (to lampoon somebody posing to be honest)

*gaye phun deoa*

To do nothing while others work.

*nake tel diye ghumano*

Sleeping with oil drops in the nostrils (to be unaware of the world around).

*chenchiye maat*

To shout down everybody.

*shukno kat khotta*

Bone dry (person with no sense of humour).

*aste piste bandhan*

Tied all over.

*panch bhute lootchhe*

Plundered by ghosts (property getting wasted).

*bhuter kertan*

Concert of ghosts (lawlessness).

*haad jvalatan*

Irritating right to the bones.

*hade hade bajjati*

Rotten to the core.

*tele begune jvale*

Fired up as brinjals in hot oil.

*aday kanch kala*

Ginger and green banana (Totally at odds).

*bhashur bhadra bou*

Woman and elder brother-in-law (Two who stay away from each other).

*bhite ghughu chadano*

To make birds roam around freely at one's house (to make one flee the house, to cause disaster).

*chhati phete yaoa*

Chest is bursting (of thirst).

*sat panch bhebe*

To think of sevens and fives (to take all aspects into consideration).

*matir manush*

Person of clay (soft natured).

*hese ajnan*

Become unconscious laughing (to dismiss as a joke).

*haste haste pet phata*

To burst laughing.

*kane tala lagano*

To deafen (A huge noise).

*ekul okul du kul yaoa*

To lose both Banks (to burn one's boats).

*hesta nesta kara*

To settle once and for all.

*pitti jvale yay*

To cause bile to burn (to be very cross).

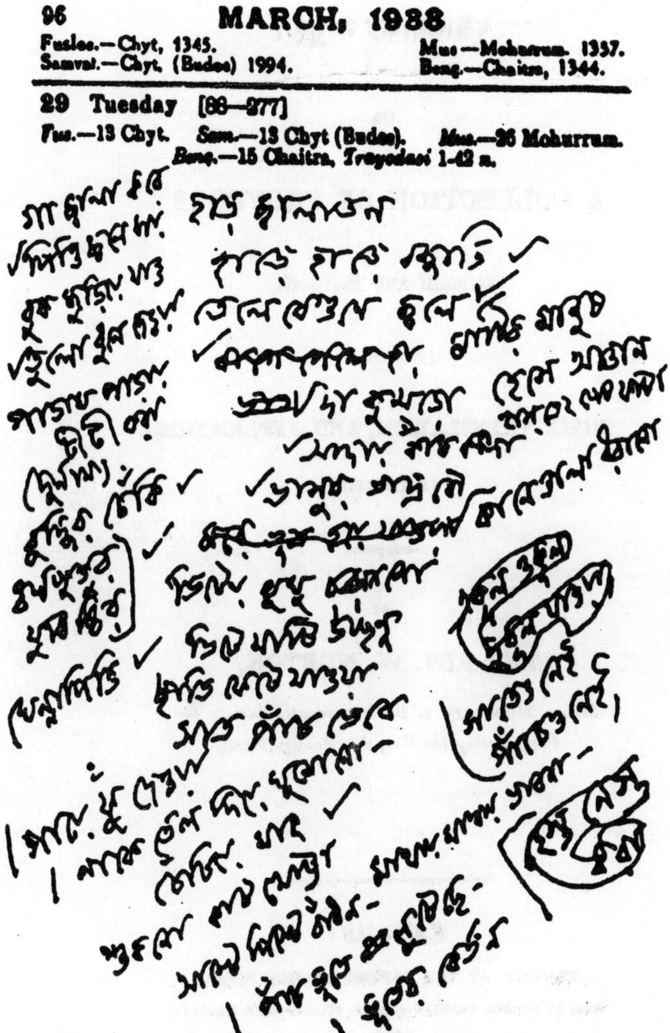

96 MARCH, 1938

Fuslee.—Chyt, 1345. Mus—Mohurrum. 1357.
Samvat.—Chyt. (Budee) 1994. Beng.—Chaitra, 1344.

29 Tuesday [88—277]

*Fus.*—13 Chyt. *Sam.*—13 Chyt (Budee). *Mus.*—26 Mohurrum.
*Beng.*—15 Chaitra, *Trayodasi* 1-42 n.

1. Rabindranath Tagore's hand writing photo copy of the proverbs which had been collected by him.

দৃষ্টান্তবাক্য সংগ্রহ ।

OR

A COLLECTION OF PROVERBS,

Bengali and Sanscrit,

WITH

THEIR TRANSLATION AND APPLICATION

IN ENGLISH.

BY

THE REV. W. MORTON,

*Senior Missionary of the Incorporated Society for Propagating the Gospel in Foreign Parts.*

---

Calcutta:

PRINTED AT THE BAPTIST MISSION PRESS.

SOLD BY MESSRS. THACKER AND CO. ST. ANDREW'S LIBRARY.

1832.

2. (*a*) The front-page of A collection of proverb Bengali and Sanskrit written and collected by William Morton.

# Preface

The Present publication arose from the following circumstances. Understanding that Mr. W. H. Pearce, of the Circular Road Press, was in possession of a series of Native Proverbial Sayings, and desirous simply of persuing them, I applied to that gentleman for the loan of his MS. who not only, in the handsomest manner, conferred the kindness solicited, but added, with a liberality that reflects upon him the highest credit, that should I feel disposed to undertake the task of revisal and translation, with a view to publication, his materials were at my diposal. The present work is the result; a work which can scarcely fail to be of service to those who study the Bengali language, whether with a view to convey instruction to the Natives themselves, or to obtain an insight into their characters, habits and modes of thinking.

The original Proverbs were, for the greater part, collected for Mr. Pearce by Natives around him. A few were kindly supplied me by my friend Mr. Reichardt. My task has been, besides correction the very numerous errors in orthography, &c. and embodying with these such additional sayings as my own reading and conversation have furnished me with, to add a translation of the whole, with a notice of the application designed, corrected and enlarged from a Bengali one attached, in most cases, to the original, and always carefully verified.

The translation aims more at correctness than elegance, which latter quality is scarcely indeed compatible either with the homeliness of most of these aphorisms, or with the literalily indispensable to the object in view in presenting them to the European public. Delicacy and propriety too. have sometimes demanded a deviation from the coarseness of the original Proverbs, which nevertheless it was judged will not to withhold, as serving to the immediate design of the publication, I must not, however, be considered responsible for any sentiments expressed, in many cases so directly at variance with the truth of nature, policy or science: my office is not to patronize opinions, but to exhibit them, in order to aid an insight into the structure of the native mind; and in doing so I trust I shall not have been unsuccessfully employed, or have expended without an adequate result of advantage, the labour, by no means inconsiderable, necessarily undergone.

The estimates formed of this collection may be various. Some may deem a large portion of its contents mean; and current among and illiterate people, the style is of course often low and incorrect; yet as the actual expression, in customary language, of the national character and notions, it is only the more valuable. Avarice and cunning, selfishness and apathy, everywhere show themselves; the sordidness of worldly aims, and indifference to higher, are seen to flow naturally from a base idolatry that confers neither elevation of mind nor purity of heart.

Hence, however, a greater sympathy with the demoralized condition and superstitious ignorance of a whole people, will probably be excited,—and consequently a more diligent and pitying activity exerted, in endeavouring to introduce amongst them the light of truth, the power of a rational piety, a holy and spiritual religion.

Nor, judging from my own experience, is the advantage small. I apprehend, derivable from this collection, towards understanding many otherwise obscure passages in books, or concise allusions in the conversation of Natives. In this view are added to the Bengali a few Sanscrit proverbs frequently heard from the mouths of the better instructed, or met with in the higher publications.

In conclusion, the merit of the suggestion of the present work is due entirely to Mr. Pearce; as well as that of having caused the far larger portion of the collection to be made—the deficiencies in execution, be they what they may, are attributable only to myself. It should be observed, however, that isolated sentences like these, and often incomplete in grammatical structure, are peculiarly diffcult and frequently susceptible of various renderings; if, therefore, I have occasionally failed to seize the just intention of a Proverb, this circumstance must plead excuse for me with the candid and considerate reader.

I now resign to the judgment of those for whose benefit I have been occupied, the result of an application, the object of which, doubtless, will obtain for my work that measure of indulgence which it may require.

**W.M.**

CHINSURA, July, 1832

2. (*b*) The preface of the book 'A collection of proverbs, Bengali and Sanskrit' (1832).

A

# COLLECTION OF PROVERBS, &c.[4]

1. উঠিত মূলা পাতায় চেনা যায়।

*The springing radish is known by its first leaf-sprouts.*

Meaning, that as the size of these decides that of the mature radish, so the future eminence or excellence of a man may be determined by the earliest indications of his disposition.

2. বাঘের গোবধ।

*'Tis the tiger's preying on the cow.*

Intimating, that if evil-disposed men injure others, or practise any villainy, it is but what was to be expected; as the natural ferocity of the tiger impels him to devour the useful cow.

3. ছুঁচো গন্ধে রক্ষা নাই, বোটকা গন্ধ কয়।

*He cannot get rid of the stench of the musk-rat, and says every thing smells rank.*

A sarcasm on one who, though wretchedly poor, yet when away from home boasts himself wealthy—as one who having in his own abode eaten something affected with the smell of the musk-rat, being invited to another's feast, supposes an ill savour in the best article of food presented him.

D

2. (*c*) The photocopy of the first page of the book 'A collection of proverbs' (1832).

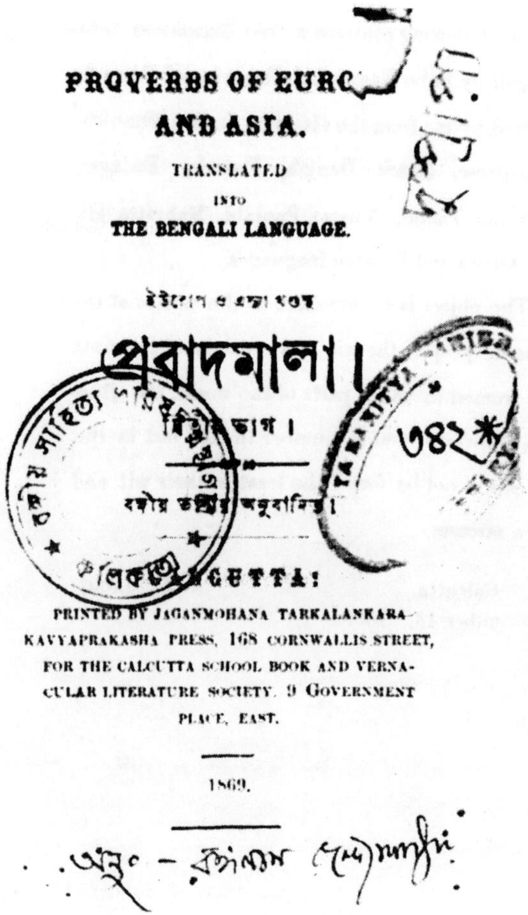

PROVERBS OF EURO[PE]
AND ASIA.
TRANSLATED
INTO
THE BENGALI LANGUAGE.

ইউরোপ ও এশিয়া খণ্ডের

প্রবাদমালা।

দ্বিতীয় ভাগ।

বঙ্গীয় ভাষায় অনুবাদিত।

CALCUTTA:

PRINTED BY JAGANMOHANA TARKALANKARA-KAVYAPRAKASHA PRESS, 168 CORNWALLIS STREET, FOR THE CALCUTTA SCHOOL BOOK AND VERNACULAR LITERATURE SOCIETY, 9 GOVERNMENT PLACE, EAST.

1869.

3. (*a*) The front-page of the second part of 'Prabadmala', a translation by Rangalal Bandopadhyay of the collected proverbs of Indian and other Foreign Languages by James Long (1869).

## PREFACE.

The following contains a free Tanslation into Bengali by Babu Ranga Lal Banerjea of Proverbs selected by me from the German, Italian, Spanish, Portuguese, Dutch, Danish, French, Badagar, Malaylim, Tamul, Chinese, Panjabi, Mahratta, Hindi, Orissa and Russian languages.

The object is to introduce to the notice of the Bengali people the wit and wisdom of Peasants and women in other parts of the world, the Russian Proverbs 200 in number though last in the series will not be found the least in their wit and keen sarcasm.

Calcutta, November 15, 1869. J. LONG

3. (*b*) Preface, written by James Long for the second part of the book 'Prabadmala', translated by Ranglal Bandopadhyay (1869).

## প্রবাদমালা।

### দ্বিতীয়ভাগ।

### জর্ম্মণীয় প্রবাদ।

১। অধিক দিন বাঁচিতে চাহ তো কুক্কুরের মত পান কর, আর বিড়ালের ন্যায় আহার কর।

২। অনুতাপই অন্তঃকরণের ঔষধ।

৩। আগুন আর জল উত্তম দাস বটে; কিন্তু প্রভু ভাল নহে।

৪। আত্মাহীন কলেবর, বারিহীন নদী, স্বামিহীন নারী, শিরঃশূন্য কলেবর।

৫। আলস্য দরিদ্রতার চাবি।

৬। আলো মাত্রেই সূর্য্য নহে।

৭। আশায় যে ভর করে, অনাহারে সেই মরে।

৮। উকীল আর গাড়ীর চাকায় তৈলচর্ব্বির প্রয়োজন।

৯। উৎক্রোশ কখন মাছি মারে না।

১০। উদর বড় কুমন্ত্রী।

3. (*c*) The photo copy of the front-page of the second part of the book 'Prabadmala', translated by Rangalal Bandopadhyay (1869).

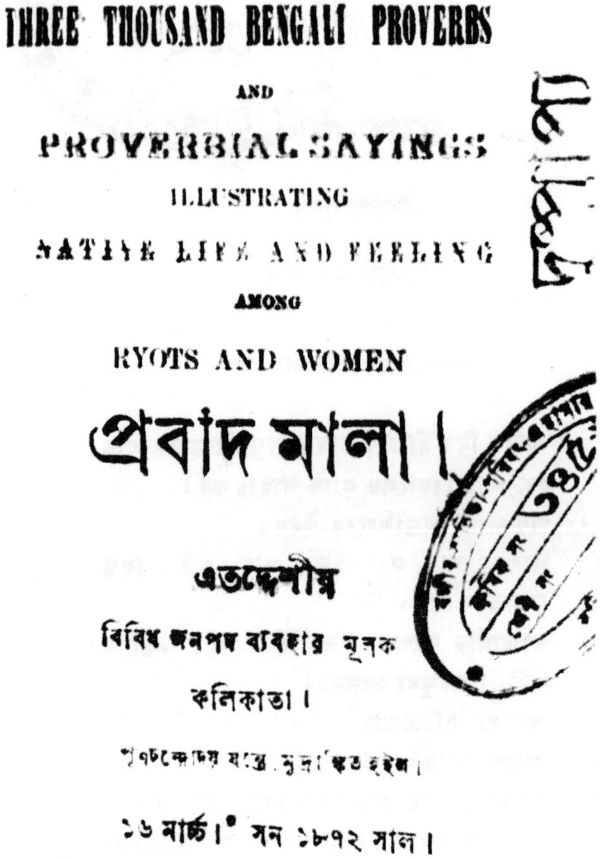

THREE THOUSAND BENGALI PROVERBS

AND

PROVERBIAL SAYINGS

ILLUSTRATING

NATIVE LIFE AND FEELING

AMONG

RYOTS AND WOMEN

প্রবাদ মালা।

এতদ্দেশীয়

বিবিধ জনপদ ব্যবহার মূলক

কলিকাতা।

প্রাচ্যেন্দোদয় যন্ত্রে মুদ্রাঙ্কিত হইল।

১৬ মার্চ্চ। সন ১৮৭২ সাল।

4. (*a*) The front-page of the book 'Proverbial Saying', collected by James Long (1872).

This little work completes the series of Proverbs and Proverbial Sayings of Bengal which I have brought out in co-operation with Pandit Nobin Chunder Bunarjyea, and other Native Gentlemen to whom I owe a deep debt of obligation for the assistance they rendered.

The series consist of about 6000 proverbs, but there are still many local sayings unpublished, and I hope some Native Gentlemen will continue my work in this direction.

J. LONG.

CALCUTTA 11TH MARCH 1872.

**4. (*b*) The Preface of the book 'The Proverbial Sayings' by James Long (1872).**

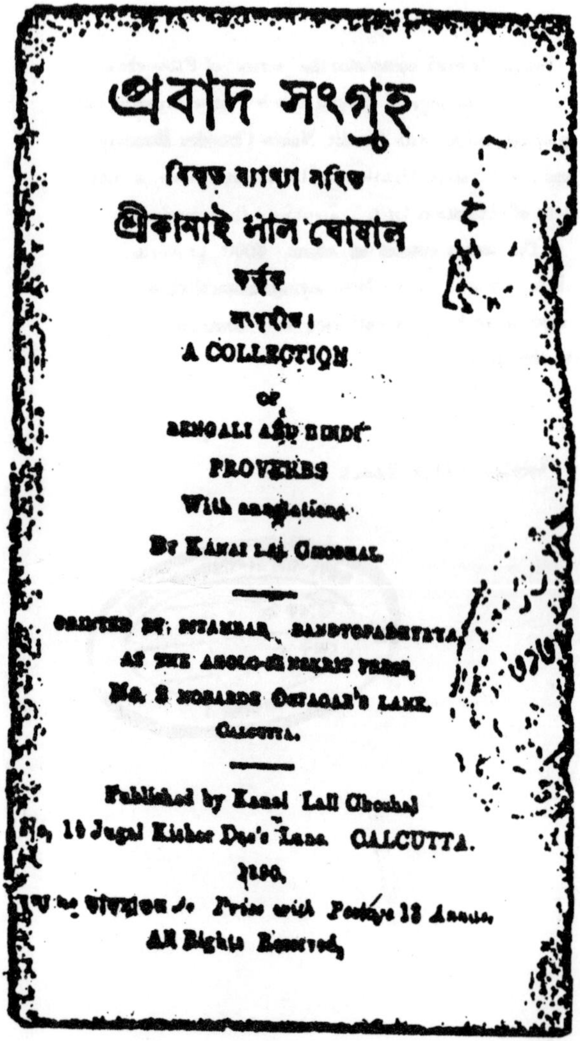

প্রবাদ সংগ্রহ

বিস্তৃত ব্যাখ্যা সহিত

শ্রীকানাই লাল ঘোষাল

কর্তৃক

সংগৃহীত।

A COLLECTION

OF

BENGALI AND HINDI

PROVERBS

With annotations

By Kanai Lal Ghoshal.

Printed by Pitambar Bandyopadhyaya,

at the Anglo-Sanskrit Press,

No. 8 Nobardo Ostagar's Lane.

Calcutta.

Published by Kanai Lall Ghoshal

No. 16 Jugal Kishor Das's Lane. CALCUTTA.

Price with Postage 12 Annas.

All Rights Reserved.

5. The front-page of the book 'A collection of Proverbs' (1896) by Kanailal Ghosh.

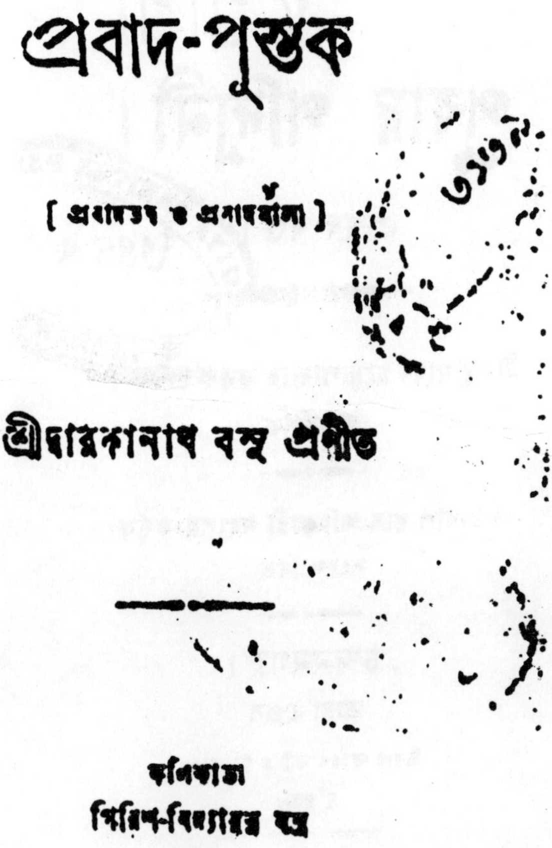

প্রবাদ-পুস্তক

[ প্রবাদতত্ত্ব ও প্রবাদমালা ]

শ্রীদ্বারকানাথ বসু প্রণীত

কলিকাতা

গিরিশ-বিদ্যারত্ন যন্ত্র

১৮৯৩

6. The front-page of the book 'Prabad-Pastak' by Dwarakanath Basu (1893).

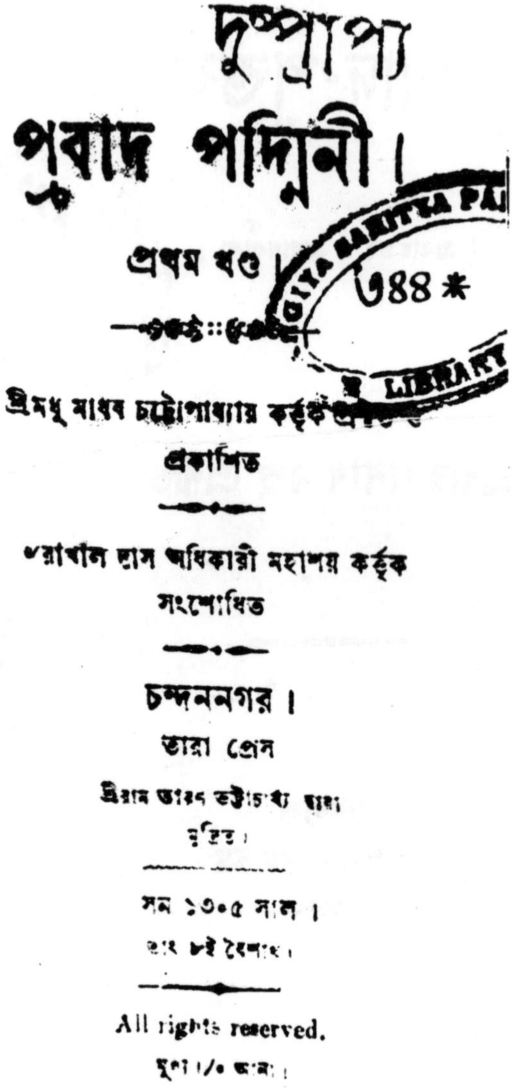

দুষ্প্রাপ্য

প্রবাদ পদ্মিনী।

প্রথম খণ্ড।



শ্রীমধু মাধব চট্টোপাধ্যায় কর্তৃক প্রণীত
প্রকাশিত

৺রাখাল দাস অধিকারী মহাশয় কর্তৃক
সংশোধিত

চন্দননগর।

তারা প্রেস

শ্রীরাম তারক ভট্টাচার্য্য দ্বারা
মুদ্রিত।

সন ১৩০৫ সাল।

তাং ৮ই বৈশাখ।



মূল্য ।/০ আনা।

7. (*a*) The front-page of the book 'Prabad Padmini', a collection of proverbs (1305) by Madhumadhab Chattopadhyay.

শ্রী...

সহায়।—

## সূচীপত্র।



7. (*b*) The content of the first part of the book 'Prabad Padmini – a collection of proverbs (4305) by Madhumadhab Chattopadhyay.

7. (c) The second page of the content of the first part of the book 'Prabad Padmini' — a collection of proverbs (4305) by Madhumadhab Chattopadhyay.

শ্রীশ্রীভুবনেশ্বরী

সহায়া—

# ভূমিকা।

বঙ্গদেশে সাধুভাষা প্রাকৃত ভাষা ও যাবনিক ভাষায় বিবিধ গ্রাম্য ও বিশুদ্ধ প্রবাদ বাক্য প্রসিদ্ধ আছে, বিভিন্ন প্রকার পণ্ডিতগণ বিভিন্ন প্রকার অর্থ করিলেও আমি বহু যত্নে যতদূর পারিয়াছি সেই সকল প্রবাদ সংগ্রহ করিয়া অশ্লীল অংশ পরিত্যাগ পূর্ব্বক স্ব-কপোল কল্পিত এবং তন্ত্র ও পুরাণাদি হইতে উদ্ধৃত করিয়া নানা উদাহরণ ও গদ্য পদ্যাদি ছন্দে ক্ষুদ্র ক্ষুদ্র প্রবন্ধে রচনা দ্বারা পরিপুষ্ট করতঃ সাহিত্য সরোবরে এই প্রবাদ পদ্মিনীকে প্রস্ফুটিত করিয়াছি। এক একটী প্রবন্ধ ইহার দলপত্র, বিদ্রূপ কটাক্ষ ইহার কণ্টকাবৃত মৃণাল ও রজ, সারগর্ভ হিতোপদেশ ইহার মকরন্দ। এক্ষণে বিচক্ষণ গ্রাহক ভৃঙ্গগণ স্বকীয় করদ্বারা রজোরঞ্জিত হইয়া প্রমোদ মধুপানে তৃপ্ত হইলেই শ্রম সার্থক জ্ঞান করিব। প্রবাদ পদ্মিনীর মর্ম্ম ভাবুকগণের মর্ম্মগ্রাহী হইলেও এরূপ প্রাঞ্জলভাবে বর্ণিত হইয়াছে যে দৃষ্টি মাত্রেই সাধারণ পাঠকগণের আনন্দ

7. (*d*) The introduction of the first page of the book 'Prabad Padmini' (4305) by Madumadhab Chattopadhyay.

অনুভূত হইবে, অথচ অতি রঞ্জিত নহে। একশত চারিটী প্রবাদে চারি খণ্ড পুস্তক গঠিত করিয়া আপাততঃ খণ্ডে খণ্ডে প্রকাশ করিতেছি গ্রাহক-দিগের সহানুভূতি পাইলে অন্যান্য খণ্ড প্রকাশ করিবার আশা রহিল। অলমতি বিস্তরেণ ॥—

শ্রীমধুমাধব শর্ম্মা।

সাং চন্দননগর

নাড়ুয়া।

7. (e) The second page of the introduction of the first page of book 'Prabad Padmini' (1305) by Madhumadhab Chattopadhyay.

# প্রবাদ পদ্মিনী।

প্রথম খণ্ড।

প্রথম সংখ্যা।

(ভৈরবীর সংসার)

তত্ত্ব জ্ঞানই এ কথার উৎপত্তির কারণ। মনুষ্য লোকে বালিকারা যেমন ধূলার ঘর নির্ম্মাণ করিয়া তন্মধ্যে কতকগুলি পুত্তলি বসাইয়া খেলা করে, সেই খেলার শেষ হইলে পুত্তলি গুলি তুলিয়া লয় এবং পদ দ্বারা ধূলার ঘর ভাঙ্গিয়া ফেলে, তদ্রূপ এই জগৎ ব্রহ্মাণ্ড জগদম্বার ধূলা খেলা মাত্র। তিনি এই ব্রহ্মাণ্ড মধ্যে মায়া রূপ ধূলায় চতুর্দ্দশ ভুবন নির্ম্মাণ করতঃ পুত্তলিকা স্বরূপ সমূহ জীব

7. (*e*) The front-page of the first part, first issue of the book 'Prabad Padmini', written and collected by Madhumadhab Chattopadhyay.

# প্রবাদপদ্মিনী।

দ্বিতীয় খণ্ড।

শ্রীমধুমাধব চট্টোপাধ্যায় কর্ত্তৃক সংগৃহীত এবং
প্রণীত ও প্রকাশিত

৺রাখাল দাস অধিকারী মহাশয় কর্ত্তৃক
সংশোধিত

চন্দননগর।
তারা প্রেস
শ্রীরাম তারণ ভট্টাচার্য্য দ্বারা
মুদ্রিত।

সন ১৩০৫ সাল।
তাং ২১ শে শ্রাবণ।



মূল্য ।/০ আনা।

7. (*g*) The front-page of the second part of the book 'Prabad Padimini' (1305), collected and written by Madhumadhab Chattopadhyay.

শ্রীশ্রীভুবনেশ্বরী

সহায়—

## সূচীপত্র ।



7. (*h*) The content of the second part of the book 'Prabad Padmini' (1305), collected and written by Madhumadhab Chattopadhyay.

শুদ্ধিপত্র।

| পৃষ্ঠা | পুংক্তি | অশুদ্ধ | শুদ্ধ |
|---|---|---|---|
| ৪৭ | ১০ | কুশুইকো | কুশুইকে |
| ৫৫ | | অপ্যায়িত | আপ্যায়িত |
| ৬৭ | ১ | পিঠেশয় | পিঠেসয় |
| ৬৮ | ১ | | ঐ |
| ঐ | ৭ | ঐ | ঐ |
| ৬৯ | ২০ | দায়গ্রস্থেরন্যায় | দায়গ্রস্থহইয়া |

7. (*i*) The second page of the content of the second part of the book 'Prabad Padmini', (1305) collected and written by Madhumadhab Chattopadhyay.

# প্রবাদপদ্মিনী।

## তৃতীয় খণ্ড।

শ্রীমধুমাধব চট্টোপাধ্যায় কর্তৃক সংগৃহীত
প্রণীত ও প্রকাশিত।

৺রাখাল দাস অধিকারী মহাশয় কর্তৃক
সংশোধিত।

হুগলী বুধোদয় যন্ত্রে
শ্রীকাশীনাথ ভট্টাচার্য্য দ্বারা মুদ্রিত।

সন ১৩০৯ সাল।

শ্রাবণ।



মূল্য ৷/০ আনা।

7. (*j*) The photo copy of the first page of the third part of the book 'Prabad Padmini' by Mudhumadhab Chattopadhyay.

শ্রীশ্রী৺ভুবনেশ্বরী

সহায়া।

## সূচীপত্র।



7. (*k*) The first page of the content of the third part of the book 'Prabad Padmini', collected and written by Madhumadhab Chattopadhyay.

7. (*l*) The second page of the content of the third part of the book 'Prabad Padmini', collected and written by Madhumadhab Chattopadhyay.

# Bibliography


Banerjee P.N. A Polyglot Book of Proverbs, Kolkata, 1996.

Barua P.C. and others: Encyclopaedia of Proverbs in 9 Vols, New Delhi, 1997.

Ben-Amos Dan: Folklore Context Essay, New Delhi, 1982.

Berman Louis A: Proverb Wit & Wisdom, USA, 1997.

Carr M.W.: A Collection of Telugu Proverbs, Delhi, 1889: Sanskrit Proverbs, New Delhi, 1999.

Castro Fidel: Neoliberal Globalization and Global Economic Crisis, NBA, Kolkata, 1995.

Chakraborty Biplab: Style in Bengali Proverbs, Burdwan, WB, 2000.

Champion Selwyn Gurney: Racial Proverbs, London, 1966.

Dalton E.T. : Descriptive Ethnology of Bengal, Calcutta, 1982.

Davidoff Hency Collected: A World Treasury of Proverbs, London, 1953.

Dundes Allan: The Study or Folklore, NJ, 1965: Folklore Matters, University of Tennesse Press, 1989.

Fallon S.M. : A Dictionary or Hindustani Proverbs, New Delhi, 1998.

Frazer Sir James George: The Golden Bough, Abridged Ed, New York, 1963.

Goldstein Kenneth S: A Guide for Field Workers in Folklore, Pennsylvania, 1964.

Islam Mazhrul: The Socio-Cultural Study of Folklore, Dhaka, 2000.

Jenson Rev. Herman: A Classified Collection of Tamil Proverbs, New Delhi, 1993.

Knowles J Hinton: A Dictionary of Kashmiri Proverbs and Sayings, New Delhi, 1985.

Leach Maria, ed: Standard Dictionary of Folklore Mythology and Legend, N.Y., 1984.

Manser Martin.H: Proverbs, New Delhi, 2005.

Manwaring A., Collected and Translated; Marathi Proverbs, New Delhi, 1993.

Mieder Wolfgang and Dundes, Alan: The Wisdom of Many, N.Y., 1981.

Mieder Wolfgang, ed: Proverbium, 18: 2001, The University of Vermont, USA.

Poczolay Gyula: European, Far Eastern and Some Asian Proverbs, Veszprem, 1994.

Rao Narasinga: A Hand Book of Kannada Proverbs, New Delhi, 1994.

Sanyal Charuchandra: The Rajbansis of North Bengal, Calcutta, 1965.

Taylor Archer: A Dictionary of American Proverbs and proverbian Pharases, USA, 1958.

Wilkins Charles translated: Fables and Proverbs, Calcutta, 1888.

**Bengali**

Adhikari Pabitra ed: Banga Sahityer Ranga Byanga, Kolkata, 2003.

Ahmed Afsar: Aloukik Dinrat, Kolkata, 1991.

Ahmed Humayun: Akash Joda Megh, Dhaka, 1988.

Ahmed Wakil: Bangla Loksahitya Prabad Prabachan, Dhaka, 1994: Lokkala Prabandhabali, Dhaka, 2001.

Alam Ohidul ed. : Chattagramer Loksahitya, Dhaka, 1963.

Angikatar Alokey Folklore, Dhaka, 1999.

Asgar Saikat ed. : Manikganjer Loksahitya, Dhaka, 1986.

Bandopadhyay Asit Kumar: Bagla Sahityer Sampurna Itibritta, Kolkata, 1378.

Bandopadhyay Bibhuti Bhusan: Aranyak, Kolkata, 1358.

Bandopadhyay Brajendranath, Das Sajanikanta ed: Tekchand Thakur: Alaler Gharer Dulal, Kolkata, 1405: Kaliprasanna Singha: Hutom Penchar Naksha, Kolkata 1404: Balendra Granthabali, 1372: Bharatchandra Granthabali, 1404.

Bandopadhyay Haricharan: Bangiya Shabdakosh, dwitiya khanda, New Delhi, 1978.

Bandopadhyay Manik: Rachanavali, Kolkata, 1384.

Bandopadhyay Srikumar, Chowdhury Biswapati ed.: Kavikinkan Chandi, Kolkata University, Kolkata, 1962.

Bandopadhyay Subhash: Loukik Aitihya, Lokayat Manas O Adhunik Bangla Kavya, Kolkata, 1398.

Bandopadhyay Tarashankar: Rachanavali, Mitra Ghosh, Kolkata, 1975.

Bangla Academy Coll. : Bangladesher Chhota Galpa, Dhaka, 1979.

Bangla Upanyase Loukik Upadan, Kolkata 1977.

Baskey Dhirendranath: Collection of Santhal Proverbs and Phrases, Kolkata 1981.

Basu Dutta Sharmila: Banglay Meyeder Bhasa, Kolkata, 2000.

Basu Jogindranath ed.: Kashiram Daser Mahabharat, Kolkata, 1315.

Basu Nagendranath ed: Ramai Pandit, Shunayapuran, Kolkata 1314.

Bhattacharya Ashutosh, Sen Dinesh Chandra ed. : Ramakrishna Kavichandra Shivayan, Kolkata, 1963.

Bhattacharya Ashutosh: Banglar Loksahitya, Vol. II, Kolkata 1963.

Bhattacharya Jatindra Mohan ed.: Ketakadas Kshemananda: Manasamangal, Kolkata, 1949.

Bhattacharya Jayashree: Banglar Prabade Nari Mon, Kolkata, 1991.

Bhattacharya P.S. pub. Brihat Khanar Bachan, Kolkata, 1315.

Bhattacharya Panchugopal: Bangla Bagdhara O Tar Bhasha Baigyanik Adhyawan, Kolkata, 1994.

Bhattacharya Sukanta: Sukanta Samagra, Kolkata, 1412.

Bhattacharya Sushil: Uttarbanger Loksahitya O Samskriti, Kolkata, 1970.

Bidyalankar Mrityunjoy: Prabodh Chandrika, Kolkata 1784.

Biswas Ranjit: Lok Aitihye Uttar Banga, Kolkata 2001.

Chakravarti Biplab: Lokavaran, Adhunik Kavitar Shaili, Kolkata 2001, Prabad Shilp Tarakashankar O Bharatiya Katha Sahitya, Kolkata 2005.

Chakravarti Nirendranath: Dekha Habey, Kolkata, 2002: Kavitar Badaley Kavita, Kolkata 1408.

Chakravarty Shibram: Rachana Samagra, Kishore, Akhanda Samskaran, Kolkata 1406.

Chattopadhya Shakti: Padya Samagra, Protham Khanda, Kolkata, 1996.

Chattopadhyay Bankim Chandra: Bankim Rachanabali, Protham Khanda, Sahitya Sansad, Kolkata, 1365.

Chattopadhyay Pashupati ed: Ramprasadi Sangeet, Kolkata, 1365.

Chattopadhyay Ramananda ed: Krittibas, Saptakanda Ramayan, Kolkata, 1353.

Chattopadhyay Sanjeev: Buno Ar Bagha Tentul, Kolkata 2000: Hanuman Tupi Kolkata 2005.

Chattopadhyay Sarat Chandra: Rachavali, Kolkata, 1995.

Chowdhury Dulal: Chakma Prabad, Kolkata, 1980.

Chowdhury Titash: Comilla Jilar Loksahitya, Dhaka, 1983.

Das Anath Nath, Roy Biswanath, Coll and ed: Rabindranath Thakur O Abanindranath Thakur Samgrahita Chhelebhulano Chhada, Kolkata, 1402.

Das Asha: Jataker Patbhumikay Banglar Loksahitya, Kolkata, 1995.

Das Asutosh ed: Dwija Ramdever Abhaya Mangal, Kolkata, 1957.

Dasgupta Tamanash Chandra ed.: Narayandeva, Padma Purana, Kolkata, 1947.

Debsen Nabanita: Chhotoder Galpasamagra, Protham Sambhar, 1411.

Devi Ashapurna: Priya Galpa, Kolkata, 1405.

Devi Giribala: Raibadi, Kolkata, 2003.

Dey Amal Kumar: Samaskrita Prabad-Prabachan, Kolkata 2000.

Dey Ranjit: Tripurar Loksahitye Janajeevan, Kolkata, 1995.

Dey Sushil Kumar: Bangla Prabad, Kolkata, 1401.

Dutta Bijitkumar and Sunanda ed: Manikram Gangulir Dharma Mangal, Kolkata, 1957.

Gangopadhyay Shyamal: Srestha Galpo, Kolkata, 2003.

Ghosh Sankha: Srestha Kavita, Kolkata 2004.

Goswami Joy: Kavita Samgraha, 2 Vols, Kolkata 2003.

Guha Bimal: Adhunik Bangla Kabitay Lokaja Upadan, Dhaka, 2001.

Gupta Kshetra O Gangopadhyay Sambhunath ed: Jyotirindranather Srestha Natak, Kolkata, 1997.

Hafeez Abdul, Choudhury Harun-ur-Rashid Mohommed: Rabindra Kavye Prabachan, Dhaka, 1997.

Haldar Jogilal ed. : Rameswar, Shivasamkirtan, Kolkata, 1957.

Halim Sardar Mohammed Abdul: Chalanbiler Lakasahitya, Dhaka, 1981.

Ijdani Roushan: Momenshahir Loksahitya, Dhaka, 1364.

Imam Ibne: Vishwer Prabad, Kolkata, 1372.

Islam Mazhrul: Folklore: Parichiti 0 Pathan, Pathan, Dhaka, 1993.

Jasimuddin: Nakshi Kanthar Math, Dhaka, 1986: Sojan Badiyar Ghat, Dhaka 1986: Bangalir Hasir Galpa, Dhaka, 1989.

Jayanti Utsav Smarak Grantha (On the occasion of 75$^{th}$ anniversary of Bangiya Sahitya Parishad) Sukumar Sen: Banglay Narir Bhasha, Kolkata, 1375.

Khaleq Muhammad Abdul: Madhyajuger Bangla Kavye Lok Upadan, Dhaka, 1985.

Khatun Manoara: Bangladesher Loksahitye Samaj, Dhaka, 2001.

Koyal Akshay Kumar ed. Krishnamurthy, Subramanian O Dey, Shyamaprasad: Nirbachita Tamil Prabad, Kolkata, 1998.

Loka Samskritir Nandantatva, Kolkata, 1996.

Long Jame : Prabadmala, Vol. II, Kolkata 1985.

Mahapatra Piyush Kanti ed. : Ghanaram Chakravarty Virochita Sri Dharmamangal, Kolkata, 1962.

Mahato Bankim Chandra: Jharkhander Loksahitya, Kolkata, 2000.

Mahato Benoy: Lokayata Jharkhanda, Kolkata, 1984.

Maji Sukumar: Unish Shatake Bangla Lok Sahitya Charcha, Kolkata, 1997.

Mandal Panchanan ed. : Gorkha Bijoy, Kolkata, 1356.

Mazumdar Manas: Loksahitya Path, Kolkata, 1991.

Mitra Devendra Nath ed. : Khanar Bachan, Kolkata, 1351.

Mitra Khagendra Nath ed. : Maladhar Bosu: Srikrishna Bejoy, Kolkata, 1944.

Mitra Khagendra Nath, Sen Sukumar, Chowdhury Bishwapati, Chakravarty Shyamapada ed. : Vaishnav Padabali, Calcutta University, 1972.

Mitra Mazumdar Dakshinaranjan: Rachana Samagra, Vol. II, Kolkata 1388.

Mitra Subal Chandra. Bangla Prabad O Prabachan, Kolkata, 1993.

Muhammad Kaji Din ed. : Loksahitya Dhanda O Prabad, Dhaka, 1968.

Muhammad Shahidullah ed. : Alaol: Padmavati Dhaka 1376.

Mukhopadhyay Bela: Bankim Sahitya O Loka Sanskriti, Burdwan: 1981.

Mukhopadhyay Harimohan ed: Gopal Uder Tappa, 1367.

Murtaza Dewan Gholam ed. Chhilte Prachalita Poi Prabad Dak-Dithan, Dhaka, 1998.

Nandi Moti: Bijolibalar Mukti O Ar Ekti Kahini, Kolkata, 2002.

Naskar Dhurjati: Sunderbaner Lok Sahitya O Vichitra Rachana, Kolkata, 1999.

Nawaj Ali: Khanar Bachan Krishi O Bangali Samskriti, Dhaka, 1396.

Pandey Tushar Kanti ed: Chanakya shloka, 700 prabad, Khanar Bachan, Kabireer doha: Mirar Padavali, Kolkata 2002.

Part II 1985.

Paschim Banger Adivasi Samaj, Kolkata, 1993.

Pathan Mohammed Hanif: Bangla Prabad Parichiti, Dhaka, 1976. Same, Second Vol. Part I 1982.

Rahman Muhammad Habibur: Bachan O Prabachan, Dhaka, 1985.

Rahman Shamsur: Shrestha Kavita, Dhaka, 2005.

Roy Biddyaddalav Basanta Ranjan ed. Bodu Chandidas Virochita Sri Krish Kirtan, Bangiya Sahitya Parishad, 1385.

Roy Chhanda O Naskar Sanatkumar ed: Gana Madhyam O Bangla Sahitya: Loka Sangbadikata O Banglar Loka Sahitya, Manas Mazumdar, 2004.

Roy Chowdhury Tapan : Bangalnama, Kolkata, 2007.

Roy Debesh: Angina, Kolkata 2000.

Roy Satyajit ed. : Sera Sandesh, Kolkata, 1391.

Roy Tarapada: Ramya Rachana 365, Kolkata 2005.

Santra Tarapada : Howrah Zilar Loka Utsav-Chhada-Prabadey Gram Banglar Samaj, Kolkata, 2006.

Sarkar Dinendra Kumar : Prabader Utsa Sandhaney, Kolkata, 1986.

Sarkar Pabitra: Loka Bhasha O Loka Samskriti, Kolkata, 1997.

Sattar Abdus : Aranya Janapadey, Dhaka, 1975.

Sen Dinanath ed. : Chattogramer Prabachen/Bagdnara, Dhaka, 1984.

Sen Dinesh Chandra, Bhattacharya Asutosh ed.: Ramakrishna Virochita Shibayan, Kolkata, 1363.

Sen Satya Ranjan : Prabad Ratnakar, Kolkata, 1950.

Sen Sukumar ed. : Krishnadas Kaviraj Chaitanya Charitamrita, Kolkata, 1963.

Sengupta Narendra Mohan ed. : Bejoygupta: Manasamangal. Kolkata, 1322.

Sengupta Pallav: Lakasamskritir Seemana O Swarup, Kolkata, 1995.

Shankar: Satdashe, Kolkata, 2003.

Sharif Ahmad ed. : Daulat Vazir Bahram Khan, Laili Majnu, Dhaka, 1357.

Sharma Shashi; Asamar Loka Sahitya, Asom, 1993.

Shastri Haraprasad ed. : Hajar bacharer Puran Bangla Bhasay Bouddha Gan O Doha, Kolkata, 1388.

Shastri Haraprasad, Sen Dinesh Chandra ed.: Manikram Ganguli, Shri Dharmamangal, Kolkata, 1312.

Shri Pantha : Thagi, Kolkata, 2004.

Siddiqui Ashraf: Loka Sahitya, Dwitya Khanda, Dhaka, 1995.

Siraj Syed Mustafa: Galpa Samagra, Protham Khanda, Kolkata, 1393.

Tagore Rabindranath: Rabindra Rachanavali published by West Bengal government on occasion of birth centenary, Kolkata 1961.

Tena Noor Mohammad, Coll & ed: Khulnar Loksahitya, Khulna, 1972.

**Bengali Journals**

Academy Patrika: Paschim Banga Bangla Academy, Kolkata, 1990.

Bamabodhini Patrika: $36^{th}$ year ($1^{st}$, $3^{rd}$, $6^{th}$ Numbers) Kolkata, 1319.

Bangla Academy Patrika: Bangla Academy, Shravan—Asvin, 1388.

Dhan Shaliker Desh: $25^{th}$ year, Second Number, Dhaka, April-June, 1997.

Ganakantha: Loka Samskriti Number, Murshidabad, 1985.

Jowar Sahitya Patrika: Chhada Special Number, Malda, 2004.

Loka Samskriti Gabeshana: Shravan-Asvin, Kolkata 1402.

Loukik Bangla (New): $1^{st}$ year, Number one, Dhaka, June, 1997.

Madhuparni: Special Cooch Behar Number, 1396-97.

Madhya Yuger Bangla Sahitya Gabeshana Patrika: $2^{nd}$ year, $2^{nd}$ Number, Kolkata.

Mijanur Rahmaner Troimasik Patrika: Pakshi Sankha $4^{th}$ year, 1-3 Numbers, Dhaka, July 1988-March 1989.

Momen Chowdhury ed. : Loukik Bangla (Ali Nawaz, Ranji Kumar Roy, B. Rama Raju: Khana Dak Ghagher Bachan O Telugu Krishi Prabad) Dhaka, 1978.

Special Darjeeling Number, 1996.

# Index

**H**



**I**



**J**



**K**



**L**



**M**